THE THREE MUSKETEERS

Borgo Press Books Edited & Translated by FRANK J. MORLOCK

Alcestis: A Play in Five Acts, by Philippe Quinault * *Anna Karenina: A Play in Five Acts*, by Edmond Guiraud, from Leo Tolstoy * *Anthony: A Play in Five Acts*, by Alexandre Dumas, Père * *Atys: A Play in Five Acts*, by Philippe Quinault * *The Boss Lady: A Play in Five Acts*, by Paul Féval, Père * *The Children of Captain Grant: A Play in Five Acts*, by Jules Verne & Adolphe d'Ennery * *Cleopatra: A Play in Five Acts*, by Victorien Sardou * *Crime and Punishment: A Play in Three Acts*, by Frank J. Morlock, from Fyodor Dostoyevsky * *Don Quixote: A Play in Three Acts*, by Victorien Sardou, from Miguel de Cervantes * *The Dream of a Summer Night: A Fantasy Play in Three Acts*, by Paul Meurice * *Falstaff: A Play in Four Acts*, by William Shakespeare, John Dennis, William Kendrick, & Frank J. Morlock * *The Idiot: A Play in Three Acts*, by Frank J. Morlock, from Fyodor Dostoyevsky * *Isis: A Play in Five Acts*, by Philippe Quinault * *Jesus of Nazareth: A Play in Three Acts*, by Paul Demasy * *The Jew of Venice: A Play in Five Acts*, by Ferdinand Dugué * *Joan of Arc: A Play in Five Acts*, by Charles Desnoyer * *The Lily of the Valley: A Play in Five Acts*, by Théodore Barrière & Arthur de Beauplan, from Honoré de Balzac * *Lord Byron in Venice: A Play in Three Acts*, by Jacques Ancelot * *Louis XIV and the Affair of the Poisons: A Play in Five Acts*, by Victorien Sardou * *The Man Who Saw the Devil: A Play in Two Acts*, by Gaston Leroux * *Mathias Sandorf: A Play in Three Acts*, by Jules Verne & William Busnach * *Michael Strogoff: A Play in Five Acts*, by Jules Verne & Adolphe d'Ennery * *Les Misérables: A Play in Two Acts*, by Victor Hugo, Paul Meurice, & Charles Victor Hugo * *Monte Cristo, Part One: A Play in Five Acts*, by Alexandre Dumas, Père * *Monte Cristo, Part Two: A Play in Five Acts*, by Alexandre Dumas, Père * *Monte Cristo, Part Three: A Play in Five Acts*, by Alexandre Dumas, Père * *Monte Cristo, Part Four: A Play in Five Acts*, by Alexandre Dumas, Père * *The Musketeers: A Play in Five Acts*, by Alexandre Dumas, Père * *The Mysteries of Paris: A Play in Five Acts*, by Eugène Sue & Prosper Dinaux * *Napoléon Bonaparte: A Play in Six Acts*, by Alexandre Dumas, Père * *Ninety-Three: A Play in Four Acts*, by Victor Hugo & Paul Meurice * *Notes from the Underground: A Play in Two Acts*, by Frank J. Morlock, from Fyodor Dostoyevsky * *Outrageous Women: Lady MacBeth and Other French Plays*, edited by Frank J. Morlock * *Peau de Chagrin: A Play in Five Acts*, by Louis Judicis, from Honoré de Balzac * *The Prisoner of the Bastille: A Play in Five Acts*, by Alexandre Dumas, Père * *A Raw Youth: A Play in Five Acts*, by Frank J. Morlock, from Fyodor Dostoyevsky * *Richard Darlington: A Play in Three Acts*, by Alexandre Dumas, Père * *The San Felice: A Play in Five Acts*, by Maurice Drack, from Alexander Dumas, Père * *Saul and David: A Play in Five Acts*, by Voltaire * *Shylock, the Merchant of Venice: A Play in Three Acts*, by Alfred de Vigny * *Socrates: A Play in Three Acts*, by Voltaire * *The Son of Porthos: A Play in Five Acts*, by Émile Blavet, from M. Paul Mahalin * *The Stendhal Hamlet Scenarios and Other Shakespearean Shorts from the French*, edited by Frank J. Morlock * *A Summer Night's Dream: A Play in Three Acts*, by Joseph-Bernard Rosier & Adolphe de Leuwen * *The Three Musketeers: A Play in Five Acts*, by Alexandre Dumas, Père * *Urbain Grandier and the Devils of Loudon: A Play in Four Acts*, by Alexandre Dumas, Père * *The Voyage Through the Impossible: A Play in Three Acts*, by Jules Verne & Adolphe d'Ennery * *The Whites and the Blues: A Play in Five Acts*, by Alexandre Dumas, Père * *William Shakespeare: A Play in Six Acts*, by Ferdinand Dugué

THE THREE MUSKETEERS

A PLAY IN FIVE ACTS

by

Alexandre Dumas, Père

Translated and Adapted by Frank J. Morlock

THE BORGO PRESS

An Imprint of Wildside Press LLC

MMX

CONTENTS

DEDICATION

To

CONRAD CADY

CAST OF CHARACTERS

- Grimaud
- Charlotte
- Claudette
- Vicomte
- An Unknown
- Georges
- Jussac
- Biscarat
- Aramis
- Madame Bonacieux
- Rochefort
- Milady
- Boistracy
- Porthos
- Valet
- Treville
- D'Artagnan
- Athos
- The King
- De Winter
- Cahusac
- Kitty
- Planchet
- Adjutant
- Black Men
- Man
- Duke of Buckingham
- La Porte Anne of Austria
- Court Clerk
- Messenger

- Cardinal Richelieu
- Officer
- Bonacieux
- Host
- Captain
- Felton
- Sentinel
- Patrick
- David
- An Usher
- Alderman
- Chambermaid
- Superior
- Masked Man
- Executioner

ACT I

Prologue

The Presbytery—A low ceilinged salon—door to the left and at rear. Window to the right, large chimney—stairway to first floor.

(Grimaud is around waiting. Charlotte descends the stairway.)

CHARLOTTE

It's well to always prepare the linen and clothes so that the carriage man can take it all in a single trip; didn't you tell me the house must be free today?

CLAUDETTE

(from her chamber door)

Yes, Mademoiselle.

CHARLOTTE

(seeing Grimaud)

Ah, it's you, Grimaud.

GRIMAUD

I'm bringing a letter from the Vicomte, the door was open. I didn't wish to call for fear of upsetting you, Miss, so I came in and I waited.

CHARLOTTE

The Vicomte usually passes by the Presbytery on his way to the hunt—why haven't I had the honor of seeing him this morning?

GRIMAUD

It's from caution! Without doubt, the Vicomte would otherwise come.

CHARLOTTE

From caution?

GRIMAUD

Yes! Yesterday the Vicomte quarreled with his father.

CHARLOTTE

With his father? The Vicomte quarreled with his father but he respects him so much—about what?

GRIMAUD

The old lord wished to present the Vicomte to Miss de La Lussaire

CHARLOTTE

Oh—to the beautiful orphan said to be the richest heiress in the country.

GRIMAUD

Exactly.

CHARLOTTE

Well?

GRIMAUD

Well! The Vicomte refused outright this presentation under the pretext that he felt no vocation for marriage. So that, not going to la Lussaire and coming here—you understand.

CHARLOTTE

Well, well—Thanks, Grimaud. Let's see what the Vicomte has to say—

(Grimaud backs away, Charlotte nods)

"Miss, the new Curé who is to replace your brother, whose lengthy absence is regarded as a renunciation of the curéship at Vitray; will arrive today." Today, the new Curé arrives—today!

GRIMAUD

Damn! Miss, it's six months since your brother left—that's a long time for Christians—six months without a mass.

CHARLOTTE

(continuing)

"But since you are staying in this house that you lived in with your brother—to leave the house today is your decision—and I advised the new Curé be lodged in another presbytery. Therefore, I will install him in a pavilion of the Château—Stay where you are without trouble or uneasiness. Believe me—very tenderly—Miss—Your devoted servant, Vicomte de la Fère."

GRIMAUD

Does Miss have a reply to give me?

CHARLOTTE

The day won't pass without my seeing the Vicomte.

GRIMAUD

Oh—very certain.

CHARLOTTE

I will wait for him then—and give my thanks viva voce.

(Grimaud leaves by the rear.)

CHARLOTTE

(alone)

Just in time; if I'd found it necessary to leave this house to pay for a new—to increase my expenses—in a month, I'd have been at the end of my resources. Thus, now this house belongs to me, poor domain. Yes, it is only a vestibule—the Château is down there—a county and a barony for three hundred years. It's almost a cruelty to have placed the window of this house in sight of the magnificent Château. There's proverb which says, "To see is to have." Lying proverb. Claudette, leave things alone. It's useless—we aren't going anymore.

CLAUDETTE

(on the pallet with linens, etc.)

We aren't going anymore!

CHARLOTTE

No, it's possible that in returning from the hunt, the Count will pass by here and be in need of refreshment—just wine and some fruits on the table.

(The old woman obeys and places fruits and a jug on the table.)

CHARLOTTE

Ah, it seems to me that crossing the woods I see a chevalier coming—oh, let him hurry, let him rush—there's a gallop which draws the cottage a little closer to the Château! The Count's Presbytery—it is well! Claudette, I don't need you anymore—go!

(Claudette leaves.)

(The Vicomte enters.)

VICOMTE

I saw you from the distance at your window, Charlotte. Why did you come in on my approach?

CHARLOTTE

As you see—to be here before you.

VICOMTE

True? Thanks.

(He kisses her hand.)

CHARLOTTE

You are very late today.

VICOMTE

I wrote to you—didn't Grimaud bring you my letter?

CHARLOTTE

Indeed—you are in good time, Mr. Vicomte, very good. I know what I say—and I answer according to my thoughts in saying that you are very good, Vicomte to offer—but excuse me, I cannot accept it.

VICOMTE

You cannot accept it! You blush to receive something from me.

CHARLOTTE

Oh, not at all, but I am leaving the country, Mr. de la Fère. It must be done. I must do it.

VICOMTE

You must refuse this house! It's necessary for you to leave the country. I don't understand you, Charlotte. Explain yourself. Why flee this country? Why run away from me?

CHARLOTTE

Because a young, obscure girl, poor and without a future—cannot be an obstacle to the glory, to the fortune of a gentleman of your name and merit.

VICOMTE

What are you saying to me, Charlotte?

CHARLOTTE

Doesn't the Count intend to make you marry Miss de la Lussaire, who is young, pretty, noble—and whose fortune will double your estate?

VICOMTE

If you know this, Charlotte, you know also that I refuse, right?

CHARLOTTE

Yes, and that's what I cannot bear—by withdrawing, I spare you the unhappiness of disobeying your father—I spare you the remorse of thwarting your fortune.

VICOMTE

Listen to me, miss.

CHARLOTTE

Vicomte.

VICOMTE

(approaching Charlotte)

Listen to me, I beg you. Here, soon after the fourteen months since you came to stay at Vitray with your brother, the year 1620 began when you arrived; I had left with the nobility of the country to enlarge the army that King Louis XIII sent to the siege of Angers against the Queen-mother. For three months you stayed in this house—after I returned to the Château, after the peace was signed by the priest of Luçon. Here, people were speaking with interest of this tender union of brother and sister.

(Charlotte gestures)

A union of all devotion on your part because the Curé Georges Backson, your brother, was of a somber humor and loved solitude. He separated you from the world in which your youth, your wit, your beauty fixed a place for you. Fraternal sacrifice on your part for—admit it—you are not happy.

CHARLOTTE

Not always.

VICOMTE

I saw you—I loved you.

CHARLOTTE

(rising.)

Vicomte.

VICOMTE

Let me continue. The most chaste virgin, the most pure young girl—can hear almost everything else I wish to say to you. You know it. For five months, you and your brother tried to withstand the advances I made to you. Silent and severe, the Abbé fled the chapel where my father and I called for him in vain. Proud and invisible, you seemed to reproach as a crime the look your eyes gave me by chance—and yet, you cannot hate me—I haven't told you that I loved you!

CHARLOTTE

Sir!

VICOMTE

Suddenly an unexpected change operates in your existence. One night this house, customarily so full of calm and of mystery, resounded with an unexpected noise—the inhabitants of the village believed they heard the hoofs of several horses. The next day, your brother vanished.

CHARLOTTE

Oh no, Vicomte—believe!

VICOMTE

I'm not asking you, Charlotte. I'm only telling you this to get where I want to go. Since then you've been alone—abandoned. I presented myself on your doorstep—because I loved you more since your misfortune. Indeed, you wanted to receive me—that was six months ago. Well—speak, it's six months since—your misfortune—. It's six months since then—well speak—for the last six months—although you've treated me with kindness and I am grateful to you for that—speak Charlotte!—Have I once held your hand without thanking you as for a Grace? Have I spoken to you a single time of love, without at the same time having sought my pardon in your eyes? Now have I ever once questioned you as to who you are: where you come from—and why your brother disappeared?

CHARLOTTE

No sir, and you've been for me as you are for all those who know you—that is to say the most loyal and generous gentleman in the Kingdom.

VICOMTE

Thanks! You understand then that it is not a vain curiosity which makes me say to you: Charlotte Backson, speak to me today with an open heart—can you do it?

CHARLOTTE

(aside)

What's he getting at?

VICOMTE

Some words about you—about your brother—about your family! A confidence to a friend, that if you wish, I will keep at the bottom of my heart, like a personal secret. Do you wish it? And I repeat, can you do it?

CHARLOTTE

(passing to the left and taking some parchments from an armoire)

About me and on my family? Here are documents that answer for me. Read, Vicomte, they will prove to you that Charlotte Backson is of good blood—if not illustrious. As for my brother—his secrets are not mine.

VICOMTE

That's fine, Charlotte. Let's not speak any more of your brother—and if we see him again—

CHARLOTTE

We will never see him again, sir.

VICOMTE

"William Backson, gentleman from Galicia—"

CHARLOTTE

My father.

VICOMTE

Anne de Breuil—

CHARLOTTE

My mother—an older brother, from her first marriage inherited all the fortune we had. My brother—the one you knew was vowed to the priesthood—and took me with him—I had lost my father and mother a long time ago.

VICOMTE

Yes—your father in 1612, your mother in 1615. Poor child.

(giving her back the papers)

CHARLOTTE

Now, you know all, sir.

VICOMTE

Then you are alone, Charlotte?

CHARLOTTE

Alone in the world.

VICOMTE

No one has rights to you?

CHARLOTTE

No one!

VICOMTE

Your heart is free?

CHARLOTTE

I thought you knew that I loved you.

VICOMTE

Repeat it to me, boldly, frankly, honestly.

CHARLOTTE

Vicomte, I love you.

VICOMTE

Charlotte Backson, will you be my wife?

CHARLOTTE

What are you saying?

VICOMTE

A very simple thing, Charlotte—since I love you and you love me.

CHARLOTTE

But your father....

VICOMTE

Listen, Charlotte—here's the sacrifice that I ask of you confidently—A public marriage would disturb the last days of my father. You wouldn't demand that of me—would you? You will accept a secret marriage?

CHARLOTTE

I am your servant, Vicomte.

VICOMTE

The day I call myself the Comte de la Fère, you will be my honored Countess. You know that my father is old, ill, suffering—you won't have long to wait, Charlotte.

CHARLOTTE

Oh!

VICOMTE

Fine. Till then we will be happy in silence and obscurity. Listen, the new pastor is coming to the Château this morning. He's one of my childhood friends. He knows of my love for you. He consents to bless our union—In an hour you will go to the church—a chapel will be lit up—I will offer you my hand, you will lend yours to it—you will swear an eternal love to me in this modest village church. Perhaps God will hear us more favorably than the oaths of kings in splendid cathedrals.

(giving her his hand)

CHARLOTTE

My lord, my husband.

(giving her hand)

VICOMTE

Here are presents from your fiancé, Charlotte—Diamonds from my mother who would bless me for choosing you—pure and noble like herself. Don't refuse me, Charlotte. As for this sapphire—it's the ring she had on her finger when giving me her eternal adieu.

CHARLOTTE

(taking the jewel box)

Your wife thanks you, Olivier!

VICOMTE

In an hour I will await you in the chapel; the clock will give you the signal. Come alone. Come as you are without more finery than you are wearing. And on my return, after I've been to greet my father as is my custom each night, the doorway of this house will become for me the most veritable palace. The lover will beg you to let your spouse in—au revoir, Charlotte, au revoir!

(kissing her hand and leaving)

CHARLOTTE

(alone—she seats herself and opens the jewel box)

Countess de la Fère!—in an hour!

(she rises)

Is it possible? Charlotte! Charlotte in your most ardent dreams of ambition, had you hoped to arrive here? Oh, I said it before—this house was only the vestibule to the Château. Claudette, bring a lamp.

(Claudette executes the order)

Good—go—Oh! In truth, if I can't see these diamonds—if I didn't feel the sapphire ring, which presses my finger, I wouldn't believe what has just come to pass.

(she tries the diamond band)

Oh! Luminous stars of the earth, constellations which shine on the faces of queens, orbs on which you raise all the splendors of this world—my hand extended for such a long while now touches you.

(A man appears at the door.)

Who is there? And what do you want from me?

(he enters)

Who are you, sir—what do you want?

UNKNOWN

Are you Miss Charlotte Backson?

CHARLOTTE

I am—and so?

UNKNOWN

You are alone?

CHARLOTTE

So you see.

UNKNOWN

A man who wanted to tell you something of importance could speak to you for a quarter of an hour without interference?

CHARLOTTE

Without doubt.

UNKNOWN

(indicating the door to the spectator's left)

This closed bolted door, doesn't it go into the room of the one you call your brother?

CHARLOTTE

Yes, sir.

UNKNOWN

(going to the left and opening the door)

Come in, fear nothing Georges, I will watch outside.

(he goes out the back, Georges enters)

GEORGES

(taking off his hat and cloak)

Charlotte, my treasure, my love, my life!

CHARLOTTE

(aside)

Him—I never thought I'd see him again!

GEORGES

Charlotte, it's me—Charlotte—answer me—don't you recognize me anymore?

CHARLOTTE

You here!

(she sits down)

GEORGES

Yes—

(on his knees)

It is strange isn't it? It's unhoped for, unheard of! Oh, I return to find you more beautiful than when I left you.

CHARLOTTE

Why have you come back?

GEORGES

(rising and leading her back to the scene)

Oh—don't ask me any questions. I don't know. I have forgotten. I see you, I speak to you. I find you again after having lost you

for six months. Oh, those six months—those six months of tor-
ture—you will make me forget them, won't you?

CHARLOTTE

Poor Georges!

GEORGES

Oh! Don't pity me; if you still love me, there isn't a happier man
in the whole world.

CHARLOTTE

Poor Georges!

GEORGES

What do you say?

CHARLOTTE

I say that you cannot stay here; that you are lost if anyone sees
you.

GEORGES

Oh, I am not here for long—I'll run and I leave again.

CHARLOTTE

(with joy)

You're leaving again?

GEORGES

Yes—listen and be happy. I am free,—you see it. I have some
money—five hundred pistoles. We will reach the sea—we will
embark, in five weeks we can be in Québec. Once there, no one
will come to ask us to account for our past. We won't dissimu-
late any more, we will fear nothing anymore—our whole life will
begin over again. Oh—the life of joy—Oh delights. You are

strong, you are courageous. We are going to leave. Come, my love, come! come!

CHARLOTTE

Impossible, Georges.

GEORGES

Why impossible?

CHARLOTTE

Five hundred pistoles—that's misery. Québec is exile.

GEORGES

Five hundred pistoles is more than we need to found a fortune—and as for exile—exile doesn't exist when one is in love.

CHARLOTTE

Yes, when one is in love.

GEORGES

My God! Charlotte, don't you love me any more? Those oaths that we exchanged?

CHARLOTTE

Many misfortunes have been caused by those oaths, Georges, which proves they were impious.

GEORGES

But, recall, Charlotte, how we are tied to each other—our love—our sorrows—our crime.

CHARLOTTE

Georges—you deceive yourself. Everything separates us—To the contrary—we are a living remorse for each other and we ought never to see each other anymore.

GEORGES

Charlotte, in the name of our love.

CHARLOTTE

(passing near the table where the diamonds are—she sits down)

Senseless love of two isolated children—lost, abandoned by God and men, and it would be to tempt heaven to think of this love again.

GEORGES

Charlotte! Charlotte!

(pointing to the jewel box)

What are these, diamonds?

CHARLOTTE

Leave, Georges—you are free—I am happy to see you free. Don't ask any more of me.

GEORGES

You are in love with another, Charlotte.

CHARLOTTE

In a half hour I'll be married.

GEORGES

Then these diamonds?

CHARLOTTE

They are the gift of my fiancé.

GEORGES

Then the one you are going to marry is rich?

CHARLOTTE

Rich and noble.

GEORGES

Oh—misfortune on me! But also misfortune on him! Name him, Charlotte.

CHARLOTTE

(rising and pointing to the Château).

He's called the Comte de la Fère—he lives in the Château. You can go find him and tell him everything, but that would be the action of a coward.

GEORGES

Is it really Charlotte talking? This terrible cold blood which freezes me to the depths of my heart—is it indeed the young girl I loved?

CHARLOTTE

No, it's the woman who has suffered.

GEORGES

(taking Charlotte in his arms)

Charlotte, will you follow me into some corner of the world where I offer to lead you where I can freely call you my wife instead of lying, as here, where I call you my sister?

CHARLOTTE

If you raise your voice like that, they will hear you—Georges, and that will be the same as if you denounced me.

GEORGES

(taking her hand and holding it to the heart)

Oh, her hand is cold. Her heart doesn't beat. You are not a woman, Charlotte. You are a marble statue—and you are right—it is madness for me to love a statue.

CHARLOTTE

Let's finish Georges—what have you decided?

GEORGES

Yes, the hour is passing isn't it?

CHARLOTTE

For you as for me.

GEORGES

Oh, for me, my resolution is taken—my future fixed. Don't worry about me, Charlotte! Oh! Now—

(at her feet)

My god—if there remained in you a heart, a single ember of your old love—if I could rekindle it under my breath—we are young—we could be happy.

CHARLOTTE

Yes—happy on your side, happy on mine. Not happy together.

(The clock strikes.)

GEORGES

What is that?

CHARLOTTE

The dark calls me—decide my destiny, Georges, I am in your hands.

GEORGES

Go Charlotte! You are free.

CHARLOTTE

Thanks—

GEORGES

On your return, you will not find me here.

(he falls on a chair)

CHARLOTTE

Thanks and adieu!

(she gives him her hand; he recoils)

GEORGES

Adieu—Madame—La Comtesse.

(Charlotte leaves.)

GEORGES

Oh! My God! My God!

(The unknown enters from the back.)

UNKNOWN

Well brother?

GEORGES

It's time! You told me so.

UNKNOWN

And now you see this woman has no soul, right?

GEORGES

I see it.

UNKNOWN

And you scorn her as the vilest of creatures.

GEORGES

I scorn her.

UNKNOWN

Good! Take your cloak—we have all night to walk. Tomorrow you will be free of all fear.

GEORGES

I will be free of it before tomorrow, brother.

UNKNOWN

What do you mean to say?

GEORGES

I scorn her, but I love her.

UNKNOWN

Georges!

GEORGES

I scorn her, but I cannot live without her.

UNKNOWN

My God!

GEORGES

I scorn her but I will die.

UNKNOWN

Die! That's a grave idea—and serious, think of it!

GEORGES

Oh! Since I am separated from her, I've been thinking of it. "Prisoner" I said to myself, "If I can escape it will be to return to her—" Free, thanks to you, brother. I told you, "Life to me is nothing without her." On the sill of her door, before going in to see her, I told you, "If she no longer loves me, I will die."

UNKNOWN

The love of a woman is a very frivolous thing in the life of a man, Georges.

GEORGES

The love of a woman is a frivolous thing for one who, besides love, has joy, riches and a future. But for one who has only this love, the love of a woman is all! Brother, you know me, I am tired of life...

(sitting near the table)

...of a life which weighs on me and on others. At the moment, the judgment which condemned me was pronounced, you made me put in my cell one of these pistols. I didn't use it—give it to me and I will use it.

UNKNOWN

Is it an unchangeable resolution?

GEORGES

Immutable!

UNKNOWN

(giving him a pistol)

Here brother, and embrace me!

GEORGES

*(the two brothers throw themselves in each other's arms—
then after stifling sighs—Georges hurls himself out of the
room crying)*

Goodbye, brother. Goodbye!

(leaving by the door on the left)

UNKNOWN

Very well. And now, Georges, the heartless woman will die like
you or will be condemned like you.

*(he puts an iron on the fire and lights a lamp, then he goes
to stand against the wall—and when Charlotte enters, he
closes the door after her.)*

CHARLOTTE

(entering by the center, looks around her)

He's gone?

UNKNOWN

Yes, but I am here.

CHARLOTTE

Who are you?

UNKNOWN

You knew me a while ago.

CHARLOTTE

Oh! Don't come near me or I'll scream.

UNKNOWN

(silence)

CHARLOTTE

Georges, Georges, help me!

UNKNOWN

Ah! You call him now?

CHARLOTTE

Where has he gone?

UNKNOWN

I am going to tell you—but first you must know from where he came—

CHARLOTTE

My God!

UNKNOWN

Georges had a good and noble heart, vowed to be a priest, he had lived for the health of the church and for others—if the demon, disguised as a young woman, had not come to tempt him.

CHARLOTTE

Ah.

UNKNOWN

A first sin committed, it was necessary to submit to the consequences. Their liaison couldn't last a long time without destroying both of them. The young girl got Georges to promise they would leave the country. But to leave the country, to flee, to reach another part of France—where they could live peacefully—that required money, which neither of them had. The priest stole the sacred vessels and sold them.

CHARLOTTE

God!

UNKNOWN

With the money, they fled, reached Berry and buried themselves in a village. But God, outraged, watched and his justice reached them or rather reached the least guilty of the two—Georges was recognized and taken to prison in Béthune and there, he took the entire fault on himself—and he wouldn't speak the name of his accomplice—he was condemned and condemned alone—to the galleys and branding.

CHARLOTTE

Condemned!

UNKNOWN

There was something terrible in all that—a thing which you are unaware of, a thing that Georges never told you—it is that his brother was the executioner, executioner of Béthune—that is to say in the village in which Georges came to be condemned—and by consequence—it was the brother who branded brother. Oh, you are unaware of that circumstance are you not? The executioner gave Georges pistols so he could blow his brains out—but the poor fool preferred to live; he loved—he lived and then—was exposed—branded and sent to the galleys.

CHARLOTTE

Horror!

UNKNOWN

Since then, the brother of poor Georges, had only one thought: to free the condemned—But once free—instead of fleeing, he wished to see the one he loved, the one who had seduced him. He came to offer her his whole life, as he had given her all his honor—she refused—But the brother remained—he had taken an oath.

CHARLOTTE

To do what?

UNKNOWN

It was that the crime should have a penalty—that the true guilty would be punished—that the accomplice of Georges, the woman whose heart killed him would be branded like him.

CHARLOTTE

But he isn't dead.

(They hear a pistol shot.)

UNKNOWN

Did you understand?

(he draws a dagger)

CHARLOTTE

(on her knees)

Oh, please, please life.

UNKNOWN

You prefer to live? So be it!

THE THREE MUSKETEERS, BY ALEXANDRE DUMAS * 35

(He quickly takes the iron in the fire and brands her shoulder.)

CHARLOTTE

Ah!

UNKNOWN

And now, do you want to know who I am. I am Georges' brother—the executioner of Béthune.

(they hear a knock on the door. He hurls himself through the window).

CHARLOTTE

(back leaning on the wall)

Ah!

VICOMTE

(at the door)

Open! It's me.

CHARLOTTE

Ah.

VICOMTE

Open it's me! It's your spouse.

CHARLOTTE

(going to the door after throwing over her shoulders a cloak which she placed on the chair when entering)

Enter, Mr. le Vicomte—your wife is waiting for you.

CURTAIN

ACT I

Scene 1

The quarters of Mr. de Treville. At night, the antechamber. The office at left. Door on the right in the antechamber leading to the Cardinal—a Musketeer on guard before the door of Mr. de Treville. A guard of the Cardinal before the door of the Cardinal. Day is coming on.

JUSSAC

(speaking to a guard at the door of the Cardinal)

Biscarat, you have the countersign. Now, remember that His Eminence loves peace.

BISCARAT

Yes, sir, Lieutenant.

JUSSAC

(looking at Aramis)

Which means that the Cardinal's guards must live in peace, even with the King's Musketeers.

BISCARAT

Yes, sir, Lieutenant.

JUSSAC

Keep your post. Mr. de Rochefort is going to relieve you.

(he leaves)

ARAMIS

You are not a lieutenant, Mr. de Biscarat, and one can speak to you under arms.

BISCARAT

Speak, Mr. Aramis, speak.

ARAMIS

I find impertinent this phrase, "even the Musketeers of the King"—and you, Mr. Biscarat?

BISCARAT

I, Mr. Aramis—I am a guard of the Cardinal, and the word does not shock me.

ARAMIS

Can one hear a bit of an explanation after guard duty, Mr. de Biscarat?

BISCARAT

That can be done, Mr. Aramis.

ARAMIS

That's all I have to say to you, Mr. Guard.

BISCARAT

I am indeed your servant, Mr. Musketeer.

(They return to walking their posts.)

(Madame Bonacieux, entering from the office of Mr. de Treville, opens the door and raps on Aramis' shoulder.)

MADAME BONACIEUX

Hush! Aunis and Anjous. Stay as you are: in front of me so the guard cannot see me.

ARAMIS

Like this?

MADAME BONACIEUX

Yes—take this handkerchief—observe the monogram and if someone presents you with the like—have confidence in that person.

ARAMIS

But when and in what manner will this handkerchief be presented to me?

MADAME BONACIEUX

At your house, Rue de Vaugirard. They will knock at the shutter. Warn the person who hides in your house.

ARAMIS

How do you know?

MADAME BONACIEUX

Suffice that I know—but that is all for the moment—the rest will come later—Take your post—Adieu!

(She goes back into the office and disappears.)

(Milady and de Rochefort leave the Cardinal's office.)

ROCHEFORT

Nothing is simpler, Milady—you will take this handkerchief— Observe the monogram.

MILADY

I see it—a "C" and a "B".

ROCHEFORT

You will go to Rue de Vaugirard—across from the carriage stop, you will knock at the shutter of a house covered with ivy, you will show this handkerchief to a person who opens the door, then you will ask the address, and as this handkerchief is the sign of recognition agreed between you—they will give you the address.

MILADY

Nothing more than that, the address?

ROCHEFORT

And you won't forget it—and you will bring it to me right away.

MILADY

A last instruction: if I am asked the name of the master of this house?

ROCHEFORT

It is a musketeer called Aramis.

MILADY

Aramis! Fine!

ROCHEFORT

Now—no sign of affection—I am going to relieve the guards.

MILADY

I am going home.

(They separate.)

ROCHEFORT

Gentlemen—seven o'clock strikes. You are free.

(Seven o'clock strikes—Milady leaves after having put a mask on her face. They relieve Aramis. A trumpet sounds. Musketeers begin to enter the antechamber—the doors open.)

PORTHOS

Eh! Yes, gentlemen, I got cold that night and as I was afraid of shivers, my word, I took my cloak.

BOISTRACY

Oh, but that's not a baldric you have there on your breast, Porthos, it's a sun.

(All exclaim in admiration.)

PORTHOS

(negligently)

It's enough, isn't it?

ARAMIS

Hello, Porthos.

PORTHOS

Eh! Hello, Aramis.

ARAMIS

In honor, you shine—come to the shadow—how's your sick friend?

PORTHOS

He suffers—the thrust was made—the sword penetrated his shoulder right into his breast.

ARAMIS

Poor Athos—is he in bed?

PORTHOS

(very loud)

With a horse's fever—happily no one knows anything—and I am not going to tell Mr. de Treville—

(D'Artagnan appears behind the group of Musketeers.)

ARAMIS

Hush! By God, Porthos, take care you have a voice like your baldric.

PORTHOS

That's true—there are some strangers here.

(D'Artagnan insinuates himself into the group, hat in hand.)

ARAMIS

Who's that there? See there, Boistracy?

BOISTRACY

He must be a Gascon freshly arrived—wait.

(going near to D'Artagnan)

Sir! Pardon.

D'ARTAGNAN

Sir.

BOISTRACY

Could I be of service to you?

D'ARTAGNAN

If you please, Mr. de Treville, the Captain of the Musketeers.

BOISTRACY

Sir, his valet de chambre is there.

D'ARTAGNAN

Sir, I thank you very humbly—

(to Valet)

Would you, if you please, inform Mr. de Treville, that the Chevalier D'Artagnan asks him for a moment of audience?

VALET

Later—Mr. de Treville is not yet here.

MUSKETEER

Gentlemen! Gentlemen! Here's the captain of the Musketeers.

ALL

Ah.

MUSKETEER

He's in a ferocious mood.

BOISTRACY

Does he already know of yesterday's little escapade?

(Enter Mr. de Treville. All the Musketeers salute him.)

TREVILLE

Good day, gentlemen, good day—eh, well, what is the news?

BOISTRACY

Nothing, Captain, nothing.

TREVILLE

The reports—the duty log.

(going into his office)

D'ARTAGNAN

He doesn't cast glances—they are pistol shots.

PORTHOS

Things are going badly.

ARAMIS

Badly!

(Porthos goes to talk to a group; Aramis stays with another in the foreground.)

D'ARTAGNAN

How glorious, the Musketeers. All the people here have faces which please me. I sense a sympathy. Wait—here's one who is losing his handkerchief.

(to Aramis, who has noticed it and put his food down.)

Sir, I believe that you were about to lose this handkerchief.

ARAMIS

(brutally)

Thanks!

D'ARTAGNAN

He isn't very friendly!

BOISTRACY

(taking the handkerchief in his hands)

Ah! Ah! Discreet, Aramis, do you still say you are on the outs with my cousin, Miss Boistracy. She is ready to loan you her handkerchiefs; see, gentlemen the initials "C.B."

D'ARTAGNAN

Oh, wonderful. I've taken a great step forward!

ARAMIS

(regarding D'Artagnan with a ferocious air)

You deceive yourself, sir. This handkerchief is not mine and I don't know why the gentlemen had the fantasy to give it to me, rather than to you—and the proof of what I say is that I have my handkerchief here in my pocket.

BOISTRACY

You deny it! That's fine for had you not, for the honor of my cousin I had been forced—

TREVILLE

(striking his fist on the table)

It's an indignity, 'S'blood!

BOISTRACY

There's the Captain who's getting angry.

D'ARTAGNAN

(to Aramis)

Sir, I am in despair.

ARAMIS

Sir, I will settle this account.

D'ARTAGNAN

Eh! If you take it that way, go to the devil.

TREVILLE

A fine report. A fine stir this will cause. 'S'blood!

PORTHOS

Heating up.

TREVILLE

We will see right now—first remove the strangers so we can discuss this business *en famille*.

(to Valet)

Who is there?

VALET

The commissary officers.

TREVILLE

Much later.

VALET

A secretary from Mr. de Tremouille.

TREVILLE

Tomorrow.

VALET

And then the signatures.

TREVILLE

Give them quickly.

(he signs some papers)

BOISTRACY

God be praised—the Captain is calm—open your cloak, Porthos, so we can admire your baldric—the King doesn't have one to equal it.

ARAMIS

I venture that this embroidery is worth ten pistoles the measure.

PORTHOS

Twelve—and it was three-quarters of a measure.

BOISTRACY

Sumptuous! The embroidery is it also fine in the back?

PORTHOS

(surrounded by the curious, envelops himself in his cloak)

Even finer.

TREVILLE

So—? Is that all?

VALET

Oh, sir—I forgot—a gentleman from Gascony—Mr. D'Artagnan.

TREVILLE

D'Artagnan—the father—my old friend, D'Artagnan?

VALET

No—sir—a young man.

D'ARTAGNAN

The son then—call him, call him.

VALET

Mr. D'Artagnan.

D'ARTAGNAN

Here!

(He rushes and knocks against Porthos, they sway together. D'Artagnan becomes entangled in Porthos' cloak, tears it—one can see that the baldric has only a front.)

PORTHOS

Imbecile!

BOISTRACY

Ah! Ah! Ah! The baldric has only a front—

(Roars of laughter.)

(He tries to pass. Porthos holds him.)

PORTHOS

You will pay me for that, Mr. Gascon.

D'ARTAGNAN

So be it—but let me pass.

PORTHOS

Oh! I will wait for you here.

TREVILLE

Well—this Mr. D'Artagnan.

D'ARTAGNAN

Here! Here!

(He enters—the laughter continues around Porthos.)

D'ARTAGNAN

Mr. Captain, excuse me, I've been very wrong to come here to you, but I have only more joy in seeing you.

TREVILLE

Thanks—a moment, young man.

(speaking low to his valet)

PORTHOS

(to the Musketeers who mock him)

It was a joke—a wager.

ARAMIS

Everything passes in pleasantry today.

TREVILLE

(continuing to read the report)

I cannot hold back any longer. Athos! Porthos! Aramis!

D'ARTAGNAN

What kind of names are these?

PORTHOS

Aye.

ALL

Aye.

TREVILLE

Athos, Porthos, Aramis.

> *(Porthos and Aramis enter Treville's office. The other Musketeers remain outside and listen.)*

PORTHOS and ARAMIS

We are here, Captain.

TREVILLE

Do you know what the King said to me, gentlemen, yesterday morning?

PORTHOS

No, sir.

ARAMIS

But I hope you will do us the honor to tell us.

TREVILLE

The King told me that henceforth he will recruit his Musketeers from the Cardinal's guards.

ALL

Oh! Oh!

PORTHOS

And why is that, sir?

TREVILLE

Because poor wine has need to be freshened up by good wine. Yes, His Majesty is right. The Musketeers make a sad face at the court, and His Eminence, the Cardinal told me yesterday how these damned Musketeers, these braggarts, these hell-raisers, loitering in the Rue de Ferou in a cabaret, a patrol of his guards, had been forced to arrest the disturbers. By God, to arrest Musketeers! Speak then, you were there. They recognized you! They named you.

PORTHOS and ARAMIS

Sir!

TREVILLE

Oh—it is indeed my fault! This will teach me to choose my men better. Let's see—you, Mr. Aramis, why did you ask the cassock of a Musketeer from me when you were so well off under a priest's robe? And you, Sir Porthos—what good does a baldric like this serve you—to hang a straw sword on it! God—and Athos, I don't see him—where is he?

ARAMIS

Sir, Athos is ill.

TREVILLE

Ill? Of what illness?

PORTHOS

They fear it may be smallpox.

TREVILLE

Here's a pretty story you create for me. He isn't sick. He was wounded, killed perhaps. If I knew it—Damnation!

MUSKETEERS

(outside)

The devil! The devil!

(they consult between them, two of them detach and leave)

TREVILLE

God's blood! Gentlemen Musketeers, I didn't know that they haunted bad places, that not ashamed of bad connections, they played with swords at the street corners. I don't wish to help the Cardinal's guards to a laugh, they are brave gentlemen—

(murmurs)

—adroit gentlemen—

(murmurs)

—men who don't put themselves in a position to be arrested and who, if they put themselves in that position, would never let themselves be arrested, I am sure. They prefer to die on the spot than to retreat! To escape, to flee, that's good for Musketeers.

(Stamping, rage outside. Porthos and Aramis gnaw their fingers.)

Ah, six guards of His Excellence arresting six guards of the King! Damnation! I've made my decision. I am going to the Louvre and I will get my dismissal as Captain of the King's guards for a lieutenancy in the Cardinal's guards. And if they refuse me, I will become an Abbé—I intend that you will be my Swiss, Porthos—you will be my Beadle, Aramis.

(Explosion of murmurs outside; D'Artagnan hides behind the table.)

PORTHOS

Eh, well, my Captain, it's true we were six against six, but we were taken treacherously and we hadn't taken our swords in our hands when two of us were killed and Athos grievously wounded.

TREVILLE

Ah, wounded.

PORTHOS

You know Athos, well, he tried to get up twice. And twice he fell. We didn't surrender, they overcame us.

ARAMIS

And I, I have the honor to assure you, sir, that I killed a guard with his own sword for they had stolen mine from its scabbard—killed or stabbed, sir, as you please.

TREVILLE

They didn't tell me that, gentlemen—and Athos?

ARAMIS

Grace, Captain, don't say that Athos is wounded—he will be in despair if that comes to the ears of the King. And as his wound is most grave he keeps to his bed—I fear—

(Athos enters, sustained by two Musketeers. He is pale as death—he opens the door and enters.

Athos.

TREVILLE

Athos. This is not prudent.

ATHOS

You asked for me is what I was told—and I hurried to obey your orders—what do you wish of me?

TREVILLE

I was just telling these gentlemen that I forbid my Musketeers to expose their lives without necessity. Brave men are dear to the King—and the Musketeers are the bravest men in the world— your hand, Athos.

(Shouts of "Bravo!" and universal joy)

ATHOS

(fainting)

Pardon, sir.

TREVILLE

What's wrong with you?

ATHOS

Pardon, sir.

TREVILLE

What's the matter?

ARAMIS

He's losing consciousness—the pain, sir—you've shaken his hand.

TREVILLE

A surgeon! Mine or better, the King's. A surgeon! Or God's blood, my brave Athos is dead.

(Everybody runs about in confusion crying "A surgeon!")

TREVILLE

Put him in this chamber here. Be careful!

ARAMIS

It will be all right. He is strong.

BOISTRACY

Eminence of the Devil.

PORTHOS

Oh! The guards of His Eminence, they are not so well behaved.

TREVILLE

Come, come, gentlemen a little space in here if you please.

(They leave and group in the antechamber.)

TREVILLE

Let's see—where was I?

D'ARTAGNAN

(timidly leaving his corner.)

Sir.

TREVILLE

Ah—that's right—Mr. D'Artagnan, well what do you want from me? I will be very happy to do something for you in memory of your father.

D'ARTAGNAN

Sir, just now I came to ask you the cassock of a Musketeer, but after what I have just seen, here I understand that such a favor would be enormous and that I don't merit it.

TREVILLE

It's good to be modest, especially when you're a Gascon. No, I cannot give you a cassock—one doesn't enter into the Musketeers except after two years on campaign or for unusual services. But there's a way to begin. Our Béarnaise cadets are not rich, and you probably are not rolling in money.

D'ARTAGNAN

(irritated)

Sir.

TREVILLE

Yes, yes, I know those arms—I am from the country. When I arrived in Paris, I had four shillings in my pocket and I fought twice with men who pretended I was not in a condition to buy the Louvre.

D'ARTAGNAN

Four shillings. I have eight.

TREVILLE

Decide—I can give you a letter to the Director of the Academy—you will be admitted without tuition—the gentlemen there learn to manage a horse—fencing and dancing.

ARTAGNAN

Oh, Sir, I know how to ride a horse. I have had my sword in the hand often enough—as for dancing—

TREVILLE

Well, you are an accomplished boy—you need nothing—come to see me from time to time to tell me of your affairs.

D'ARTAGNAN

(aside)

I'm getting my dismissal.

(aloud)

Ah, sir—I don't know how to speak to you. You disturb me and I lose my head. Why don't I have my father's letter? His recommendation was much needed today.

TREVILLE

In fact—why is it you came here without his letter of recommendation?

D'ARTAGNAN

Eh! I had one, Sir, a fine one, but it was perfidiously stolen from me.

TREVILLE

Stolen?

D'ARTAGNAN

Yes, Sir, at Meung—in a hostel—I was riding a yellow horse.

TREVILLE

You were riding a yellow horse.

D'ARTAGNAN

Button of Gold—a gentlemen there pretended that the creature belonged to the realm of vegetables rather than the kingdom of animals. We put swords in our hands. But the host came in and his servants cowardly fell on me with blows from a stick. They wounded me, Sir, wounded me despite the threats I made invoking your name.

TREVILLE

My name! You spoke aloud of me?

D'ARTAGNAN

What do you expect! A name like yours ought to serve me as a shield—all the length of my journey I announced myself as the protégé of Mr. de Treville, but fate declared against me. My adversary left me prisoner of the valets.

TREVILLE

A gentleman? That's bad.

D'ARTAGNAN

He had a sort of excuse. He was waiting on a lady—a beautiful lady who came,—in fact with whom he had a long conversation—But it wasn't a reason to question the Host about me, to search my pockets after they had undressed me—apparently to dress my wound, but in reality to steal my father's letter for without any doubt, it was he who robbed me.

TREVILLE

For what motive?

D'ARTAGNAN

Eh! Jealousy, I suppose.

(Reentry of Aramis and Porthos.)

TREVILLE

Hum! You say this happened at Meung?

D'ARTAGNAN

Yes, sir.

TREVILLE

When was that?

D'ARTAGNAN

Eight days ago.

TREVILLE

And that this gentleman was waiting on a lady?

D'ARTAGNAN

A very beautiful woman.

TREVILLE

Was this man high-waisted?

D'ARTAGNAN

Yes.

TREVILLE

Tanned complexion—black mustache?

D'ARTAGNAN

Yes, that's him.

TREVILLE

A scar on his face?

D'ARTAGNAN

Exactly. But how is it you know this man? Ah, if I ever find him. Ah, Sir, find him for me, I beg you.

TREVILLE

What did this woman say to him? Do you know?

D'ARTAGNAN

She told him, "Run, announce down there that he will be in Paris in eight days."

TREVILLE

And did he reply?

D'ARTAGNAN

He replied—"Yes, Milady".

TREVILLE

It's him, it's him—the two of them. Ah! Your Eminence the Cardinal—let's see, young man, let's think of you.

D'ARTAGNAN

Sir, you have just said that you know this man—well I absolve you of all your promises, I release you of your kindnesses. Only tell me only his name—his name! I intend to be avenged. I am burning.

TREVILLE

Protect yourself! If you see him come one side of the street, cross to the other. Don't strike against the rock, you will break like glass! Let's see, be calm, Gascon that you are, while I go to write to the Director of the Academy.

D'ARTAGNAN

That's good. That's good. Just let me find him again! Rock or sponge—if he falls into my hands—

(he looks out the door)

Ah!

TREVILLE

Well, what?

D'ARTAGNAN

Eh—but it's him!

TREVILLE

Who?

(Rochefort, leaving the Cardinal crosses the stage.)

D'ARTAGNAN

My traitor, my thief.

TREVILLE

Stop! Ah, my word, go to the devil!

D'ARTAGNAN

(rushing)

Wait! Wait!

(D'Artagnan leaving, bumps into Athos.)

ATHOS

'S'blood!

(He puts his hand on his shoulder)

D'ARTAGNAN

Pardon! I'm in a rush.

ATHOS

You are in a rush?

(stopping D'Artagnan)

And that pretext suffices for you?

D'ARTAGNAN

The wounded Musketeer. Yet another stupidity! Excuse me, sir—I—

ATHOS

A moment! You are not Mr. de Treville to treat Musketeers cavalierly.

D'ARTAGNAN

My word, sir. I did not mean to bump into you and I said "Excuse me." I find that should suffice—I am in a rush, word of honor!

ATHOS

I understand that you may be in a hurry.

D'ARTAGNAN

Oh! It's not to escape—I am running after someone.

ATHOS

Well, Mr. Man-in-a-Hurry—you will find me without running— do you hear?

D'ARTAGNAN

Where's that, if you please?

ATHOS

Near Carmes fields.

D'ARTAGNAN

At what time?

ATHOS

At noon—and try not to make me wait, for at 12:15 I will be running after you and will slice off your ears.

D'ARTAGNAN

I will be there at ten minutes to noon.

(Athos releases him—he starts to run.)

PORTHOS

(in a group)

Mr. Gascon.

D'ARTAGNAN

The man with the baldric—Hell!

PORTHOS

Do you know the Luxembourg?

D'ARTAGNAN

I will make its acquaintance.

PORTHOS

At noon.

D'ARTAGNAN

Not at all. At one o'clock if you please.

PORTHOS

So be it!

D'ARTAGNAN

And so two! By running fast I may yet catch my thief.

(He starts running again.)

ARAMIS

(near the door)

Sir!

D'ARTAGNAN

Ah fine! The man with the mustache!

ARAMIS

You know that I will be waiting for—at noon, Rue du Chasse Midi.

D'ARTAGNAN

No, sir, at two o'clock, if it's the same to you.

ARAMIS

Two o'clock! So be it!

D'ARTAGNAN

Well—here I am sure of my business. Three chances to be killed today—yes—but I will be killed by a Musketeer. That will be pretty. Still, if I can kill my thief before noon! Bah—let's try.

(He goes running and disappears.)

AN USHER

(in Treville's apartment)

The King.

THE KING

(entering)

Good day Treville, are you reconciled with the Cardinal? I am going to him.

TREVILLE

Reconciled with the Cardinal? Me?

THE KING

Certainly, you must be. His guards beat our Musketeers.

TREVILLE

Oh!

THE KING

Goodbye, Treville.

TREVILLE

The King, gentlemen.

(Drums. Guards on duty present arms, the others line up. The King leaves.)

CURTAIN

ACT I

Scene 2

The entrance to the Carmes fields; an arid meadow, old bastions without windows—on one side the background is empty of houses.

ATHOS

(seated on a milestone)

Nobody! My Gascon won't be coming? Let's wait.

D'ARTAGNAN

(arriving all out of breath)

Ah, Sir, you are the first at our rendezvous. Excuse me—it's because I've been running so much and couldn't find anything. Oaf! Whoo!

ATHOS

It's not yet noon, sir, you're not yet late.

D'ARTAGNAN

There's noon sounding.

ATHOS

Sir, I have advised my two friends who will serve me as seconds—but these two friends are not yet come, at the same time I don't see yours.

D'ARTAGNAN

I don't have any, sir—arrived only yesterday at Paris, I don't know anyone except Mr. de Treville and besides—

ATHOS

You don't know anyone? Ah, but then if I kill you—what a misfortune—I will seem to be a devourer of children.

D'ARTAGNAN

Not at all, sir, because you are at a disadvantage since you do me the honor of drawing a sword against me with a wound which must inconvenience you very much.

ATHOS

Very inconvenienced, on my oath! You caused me a devilish pain—but as I am very tired on my right-hand side—I will use my left—It's my custom on such occasions—oh, I'm not giving you any grace—I use either hand equally well and the advantage is perhaps mine—a lefty is very irritating to those who are not used to one.

D'ARTAGNAN

Oh, sir, don't worry about me, I beg you. I'm not worth the trouble—let's talk about you.

ATHOS

You confuse me—but these gentlemen are not coming. Oh God's Blood—how you hurt me! My shoulder is burning.

D'ARTAGNAN

If you would permit me, sir—I have a miraculous balm which comes from my mother—I would give you some, and I am sure in three days this balm would cure you.

ATHOS

Really?

D'ARTAGNAN

Really—in about three days, when you are cured, it would be a great honor to me to be your man.

ATHOS

By the Lord—there's a proposal that pleases me—it shows a man of heart. Thanks, but three days from now, you see, the Cardinal or his men will know that we must fight each other and they will oppose our conduct—ah, but these loafers haven't come yet.

D'ARTAGNAN

If you are in a hurry, sir, and it pleases you to expedite things with me right now, don't upset yourself.

ATHOS

There's another thing I find agreeable, he isn't a man without a brain. Sir, I love people of your mettle and if we don't kill each other today—I believe that later, I will have a real pleasure in your conversation. Ah—here's one of my men.

D'ARTAGNAN

What Mr. Porthos?

ATHOS

Does that annoy you?

D'ARTAGNAN

Not at all.

PORTHOS

Ah, what do I see?

ATHOS

It's with this gentleman that I am fighting.

PORTHOS

And I, too.

ATHOS

You, too?

D'ARTAGNAN

At one o'clock.

ARAMIS

(arriving)

And I, too—I am fighting with this gentleman.

D'ARTAGNAN

At two o'clock.

ARAMIS

That's true—but why are you fighting, Athos?

ATHOS

My word, I don't know. He hurt my shoulder and you, Porthos— why are you fighting with this young man?

PORTHOS

I am fighting because—I am fighting.

D'ARTAGNAN

A discussion over toiletry.

ATHOS

But you, Aramis—what's your quarrel with him?

ARAMIS

A point of courtesy.

(to D'Artagnan)

Sir?

D'ARTAGNAN

About Saint Augustine, yes.

ATHOS

(aside)

This a boy with spirit—decidedly.

PORTHOS

Then let's take our turn.

D'ARTAGNAN

One moment, gentlemen, at present you are reunited—permit me
to make my excuses—

ALL

Oh—oh.

D'ARTAGNAN

You don't understand me—I excuse myself for only one thing—
and that's for not being able to pay my debt to all three of you. In
fact, Mr. Athos has the right to kill me first, which much deval-
ues the worth of your claim, Mr. Porthos, and renders yours almost null, Mr. Aramis. I will become a bankrupt by one of you
or perhaps two. That's what I would excuse, nothing more—
Now, gentlemen, whenever you wish.

ATHOS

Right now.

D'ARTAGNAN

I will die! But—even if a hundred Musketeers came on together, I won't retreat a step.

(They draw their swords.)

ATHOS

You've taken a bad position. You have the sun in your eyes.

D'ARTAGNAN

Bah! I knew it—I am from the Midi.

(They begin to duel.)

(Enter Jussac, Biscarat, De Winter, Cahusac and guards.)

JUSSAC

Oh! Oh! Musketeers; are they fighting here? And the edicts that we made?

ATHOS

Jussac.

PORTHOS

The Cardinal's men.

ARAMIS

Sheath your sword.

JUSSAC

It is too late.

ATHOS

Eh! Gentlemen—why are you meddling? If we saw you fighting, killing yourselves, I tell you, we wouldn't prevent you.

BISCARAT

Always agreeable. The lessons didn't profit you, it appears?

ARAMIS

Ah, Mr. Biscarat, you remind us that we have an intimate game.

JUSSAC

More provocations! We are on duty, gentlemen, put up your swords and follow us.

ARAMIS

Impossible to obey your gracious invitation. Mr. de Treville has forbidden us—

JUSSAC

Is it like that?

ATHOS

Yes, indeed, it's like that.

JUSSAC

Well—if you won't obey us—

ATHOS

What?

JUSSAC

You're going to see. Look here, the rest of you! Mr. de Winter, you are not one of the Cardinal's men, you are English, if you wish to absent yourself—

DE WINTER

No, gentlemen, I am not one of the Cardinal's men but my sister, Lady de Winter, is one of the friends of His Eminence. I am English, it is true, but more reason for me to show some French men that one fights as well in England as in France, and as my walk has brought me here, what you do, I will do.

ATHOS

(to his friends)

They are five—we are three, we will still fight and if necessary, we will die here. For, I tell you I will never again appear defeated before the Captain.

PORTHOS

Nor I.

ARAMIS

Nor I—

D'ARTAGNAN

(in a corner)

Here's the moment of decision. If I don't deceive myself it's one of those events which decide the life of a man. It's a question of choosing between the King and the Cardinal. No sadder friend than the King, no ruder enemy than the Cardinal—Oh! Bah! I have the heart of a Musketeer. So much the worse. Pardon, gentlemen.

ATHOS

What?

D'ARTAGNAN

You just made a mistake in saying you were only three.

ARAMIS

But no.

PORTHOS

We are three!

JUSSAC

The devil—are they taking reinforcements? Come on you others. Sword in hand, on a line. You, handsome Gascon, decamp—we have given you the key to the field—save your skin!

BISCARAT

You will do wisely for there's going to be a shower of sword blows.

D'ARTAGNAN

Well—it can rain for all the world—I'm staying.

ATHOS

You side with us against them? You—our enemy? That's handsome, but—

D'ARTAGNAN

Yes—I see—you wonder if I'm worthy of my man. Try, always try—I will do well enough to die properly.

ATHOS

Come on, you're a pretty fellow. What's your name?

D'ARTAGNAN

D'Artagnan.

ATHOS

Well—Athos, Porthos, Aramis, and D'Artagnan, charge.

JUSSAC

Ah, is that what you intend. Well—you others, charge, charge.

ALL

Charge.

(General fighting.)

D'ARTAGNAN

(after having crossed swords with Jussac, to de Winter)

If you want, there's a place for everybody.

DE WINTER

No—I will replace the first one who is wounded.

PORTHOS

(to Cahusac)

Didn't I just hear 12:30 sound, Mr. de Cahusac?

CAHUSAC

Braggart!

PORTHOS

You have a pretty blade, my dear boy.

ARAMIS

(to Biscarat)

Biscarat, I owe you this.

(he kills him)

Someone else.

JUSSAC

That's a provincial way you have there.

D'ARTAGNAN

A Gascon trick, yes, sir.

(he wounds him)

ATHOS

(to Aramis)

He does well, this D'Artagnan.

ARAMIS

And you, Athos?

ATHOS

Me—I—I—suffer—but I'm healing up.

D'ARTAGNAN

Wait on me a little.

JUSSAC

He's charming—that one.

D'ARTAGNAN

Aren't I? Come—

(he overthrows Jussac)

That's a thrust from Mr. D'Artagnan Senior—Mr. de Winter, I am at your orders.

ATHOS

Leave him to me. It's he who wounded me yesterday.

(Athos disarms one of the guards.)

PORTHOS

(touching his man)

Three to four.

ATHOS

(to the guard he has just disarmed)

Surrender!

D'ARTAGNAN

I will kill you.

(to De Winter)

DE WINTER

Kill!

D'ARTAGNAN

My word, no—you show me a brave Englishman, you will live.

DE WINTER

Thanks! Your name, sir? Your address.

D'ARTAGNAN

If it's to start over again, I am here—let's start right now.

DE WINTER

No, sir—it's to thank you—it's to present to my sister a gallant man to whom I owe my life—thus—I ask your name and your address.

D'ARTAGNAN

The Chevalier D'Artagnan, Rue des Fossoyeurs.

DE WINTER

Sir, receive all my compliments. Till we meet again.

PORTHOS

Ah! Ah! There's a return match.

D'ARTAGNAN

(seeing the Musketeers leaving without him)

And me?

ATHOS

You? You? Embrace me—and don't hurt my shoulder.

(Aramis and Porthos embrace D'Artagnan.)

D'ARTAGNAN

We are then friends?

ATHOS

For life—till death!

ALL

For life—till death!

ATHOS

Only you're going to have trouble with the Cardinal.

D'ARTAGNAN

Oh, bah! If I am accepted as an apprentice Musketeer. The Cardinal isn't my uncle.

CURTAIN

ACT I

Scene 3

At Milady's.

> *(Rochefort enters before Kitty.)*

KITTY

No, sir, you cannot enter. No one comes into Madame's apartment.

ROCHEFORT

> *(crossing the stage)*

Then, my pretty child, you who can enter—announce Mr. de Rochefort—go at once.

KITTY

I—I cannot enter any more than you—when Madame is dressing.

ROCHEFORT

Ah, that's right—an Englishwoman. But how does one speak to an English lady when one is in a hurry?

KITTY

I am going to ring Madame.

> *(she rings)*

ROCHEFORT

The other way around in France.

KITTY

But here it's like this.

ROCHEFORT

Oh—this mustn't last long!

KITTY

The gentleman is in a rush?

ROCHEFORT

Very much in a rush.

(Kitty rings again and leaves at the back. Enter Milady.)

MILADY

Ah, it's you Rochefort—well, do you bring me news of Lord de Winter?

ROCHEFORT

Of Lord de Winter? No—why?

MILADY

It seems he was in a fight between the Cardinal's guards and some Musketeers.

ROCHEFORT

Well—what do you see there so frightening? There's one almost every day.

MILADY

Without doubt, but my brother—Lord de Winter is not always mixed up in these fights.

ROCHEFORT

And they fought today?

MILADY

Here's what happened—Lord de Winter was walking with the guards—they met some of Treville's Musketeers—and then blood was shed!—my brother was perhaps killed!

ROCHEFORT

Oh, my God—but how do you know this, Milady?

MILADY

My brother's valet saw them engage from a distance—he ran here totally frightened, poor boy.

ROCHEFORT

You sent him to warn the Cardinal?

MILADY

No, I lost my head. I don't know what I did.

ROCHEFORT

Oh, you were wrong to despair—the baron is not your brother.

MILADY

He's only the brother of the old Lord de Winter, my husband, but it doesn't matter. I love him a lot.

ROCHEFORT

This poor baron! I don't know why but something tells me he's suffered a misfortune.

MILADY

You think so?

ROCHEFORT

These devilish Musketeers have such happy or rather such unfortunate hands—after this—there's a single consolation.

MILADY

Which is?

ROCHEFORT

If the baron is killed, his fortune won't be lost.

MILADY

Why?

ROCHEFORT

He had one hundred thousand shillings of revenue—right?

MILADY

A bit less.

ROCHEFORT

Well—doesn't your son, his nephew, inherit from him?

MILADY

Oh, Count, this isn't what you came to tell me is it?

ROCHEFORT

Pardon—you know how practical I am—but let's leave Lord de Winter's inheritance—no, it's not for that I came to speak to you.

MILADY

Speak then.

ROCHEFORT

I came to explain to you all our plans for the kidnapping of Lord Buckingham!

MILADY

Let's see.

ROCHEFORT

After showing the handkerchief in the Rue de Vaugirard, the address was given to you, right.

MILADY

Yes—then?

ROCHEFORT

The address discovered, you will indicate a rendezvous to the Duke.

MILADY

Quite right. At what place?

ROCHEFORT

At the home of this little Bonacieux, the confidante of the Queen,—the Duke will give himself up without suspecting.

MILADY

Evidently.

ROCHEFORT

And we have established a mousetrap at the home of this little Bonacieux.

MILADY

A mousetrap?

ROCHEFORT

Yes—we in Paris call a mousetrap the place where the mice always enter, but from which they never leave.

MILADY

I understand.

ROCHEFORT

You will see that the Duke is taken and taken at the home of Bonacieux, the confidante of the Queen. That's what must be demonstrated as they say in geometry.

MILADY

That's understood—till this evening—now let me inform myself.

ROCHEFORT

Ah, yes—of the succession—pardon, of the situation of Lord de Winter.

KITTY

(entering)

Lord de Winter, Milady.

MILADY

Ah—wounded?

ROCHEFORT

Mortally?

(Enter de Winter.)

DE WINTER

Good day, Milady, good day, sister.

MILADY

Ah! Sir, I was in such an anxiety.

ROCHEFORT

I witnessed it, dear Count, Madame thought you were dead.

DE WINTER

I would have been, Mr. de Rochefort, but for the generosity of my adversary, who nobly gave me my life.

ROCHEFORT

A handsome trait, isn't it, Madame, a handsome trait?

MILADY

Oh—magnificent.

DE WINTER

So handsome, that I begged this cavalier to come with me that I might present him to you, my sister.

MILADY

And he came?

DE WINTER

He is below—do you permit me to show him up?

MILADY

Without doubt—I will be charmed—who is this cavalier?

DE WINTER

A gentleman from Béarn, the Chevalier D'Artagnan.

MILADY

My Gascon!

ROCHEFORT

My Gascon. He mustn't find me here—Milady—Milady—pardon, Count—Milady, don't you have here somewhere a hidden door?

MILADY

There it is.

(pointing to a door on the side)

ROCHEFORT

Fine—permit me to disappear.

(aside leaving)

I was sure she had a secret door.

MILADY

What's wrong with him? Well, I am waiting for your conqueror, my brother.

DE WINTER

Chevalier! Chevalier! Enter, I beg you.

(He comes in very suspicious, constantly looking behind him.)

D'ARTAGNAN

(aside)

I just saw a man who crossed the Court—a man! It's singular, I sense my thief.

(Having looked out the window he returns to the corridor.)

DE WINTER

You see, Madame, the gentlemen who preserved to you a brother—thank him then—if you have some friendship for me.

MILADY

(aside)

Cursed Gascon.

(aloud)

Be welcome, sir. Today you have acquired eternal rights to my recognition—but what's the matter then?

D'ARTAGNAN

Pardon, Madame—it's that I always think—ah—Milady.

DE WINTER

Well, what?

MILADY

Singular manner of presenting oneself!

D'ARTAGNAN

Excuse my distraction, Madame—and you too, Milord, Madame is so beautiful.

MILADY

One excuses all, even without a compliment on the part of a man as brave and as generous as you are, Mr. D'Artagnan. I love warlike prowess very much and if you wish to satisfy me completely—you will recount your combat to me.

D'ARTAGNAN

Ah, Madame—and modesty?

DE WINTER

I will speak then, since you are modest—but first here's some Cyprian wine and some glasses—you're going to do me right—aren't you, Milady?

MILADY

Certainly.

(De Winter pours some wine.)

D'ARTAGNAN

It's singular—I would have thought his so-tender sister would have jumped at my throat, and devoured me with caresses—and not at all—one would say she was looking at me sideways—oh what eyes!

DE WINTER

To your health, Chevalier—my sister.

D'ARTAGNAN

What a shame that such pretty eyes are so naughty.

(he drinks)

DE WINTER

Sit, my friend, sit, I beg you—now, sister, I am ready for my recital. Ah—it was a rough combat, nine well-sharpened swords were interlaced, twisted like snakes to the sun.

KITTY

Milord—a little lackey is waiting for you in the vestibule. His mistress, he says, is very uneasy about Your Honor.

DE WINTER

Ah, it's true, poor woman. Permit me, my sister, permit me, Mr. D'Artagnan. I leave you in each other's good company—without goodbye, Chevalier—come, Kitty.

D'ARTAGNAN

Devil of an Englishman! To leave me alone with this woman! So much for doing someone a good turn!

MILADY

Well, sir, don't you talk?

D'ARTAGNAN

But Madame, truly, I am so afraid of being indiscreet.

MILADY

Why, then, Mr. D'Artagnan? You are timid?

D'ARTAGNAN

My word, Madame, more than timid. I am embarrassed.

MILADY

And you admit it?

D'ARTAGNAN

Oh—if I admitted nothing to you—you would perceive every-thing. I prefer to admit it—that makes me speak and emboldens me a little.

MILADY

Mr. D'Artagnan, it's wrong for you to be timid. It will injure you very much.

D'ARTAGNAN

In what way, Madame?

MILADY

Valiant, young, brave—soon you will have a reputation—with a reputation, successes—

D'ARTAGNAN

You believe so?

MILADY

It's inevitable—at least if you're not of an amorous humor.

D'ARTAGNAN

Oh, Madame—much to the contrary.

MILADY

Ah! You are—

D'ARTAGNAN

Yes, Milady—yes, and if I found—

MILADY

What?

D'ARTAGNAN

(trying to take her hand)

If I found a little indulgence.

MILADY

Pardon, Mr. D'Artagnan—aren't you trying to find service to take in Paris?

D'ARTAGNAN

She's changing the conversation—it's a shame, I was starting out—

(aloud)

Service in Paris?

MILADY

Without doubt; you have some friends.

D'ARTAGNAN

I have three—three Musketeers.

MILADY

But you cannot join the Musketeers—it's very difficult. Don't you have a bit of ambition?

D'ARTAGNAN

That can be seen.

MILADY

What about a very high service, very brilliant—the service of His Eminence, for example.

D'ARTAGNAN

Ah, I cannot, Madame—my three friends are embroiled with the Cardinal—and I myself—because of this fight—

MILADY

I understand, oh, His Eminence has so much trouble—oh, indeed—but I am not proposing you for the service of the Cardinal, Mr. D'Artagnan, I was being very officious.

D'ARTAGNAN

Oh, Madame, it's not that I disdain the service of the Cardinal—I have great admiration for His Eminence—but it's been brought home to me that the office of the Louvre and the Palace of the Cardinal are often picking a fight with each other—and in my position and in that of my friends—who can foresee if His Majesty and even Mr. de Treville—one day—well, never mind, I am wading into politics—I much prefer the first conversation, Milady.

MILADY

Mr. D'Artagnan!

D'ARTAGNAN

Milady, I was by way of saying just now that if I found an indulgent soul, I would force myself to be neither too indiscreet nor too timid.

MILADY

(aside)

He's the one who changes the conversation this time—not bad, in truth—I will speak of this clown to the Cardinal.

D'ARTAGNAN

You don't reply, Madame?

MILADY

In truth, sir, what can I reply to you—you make me a point-blank declaration.

D'ARTAGNAN

A declaration? Well, Madame, resist it.

MILADY

You are very dangerous, Chevalier.

(aside)

He's just cost me a hundred thousand pounds rent and he pays court to me—oh, I will watch him.

(aloud)

Mr. D'Artagnan, a garrison so vigorously besieged has only one resource.

D'ARTAGNAN

Which is?

MILADY

To make a sortie.

D'ARTAGNAN

Oh, Madame, you are leaving me? You're angry with me?

MILADY

I am not angry with you, but I am going to hide. Goodbye, Chevalier.

(Exit Milady.)

D'ARTAGNAN

Well, I hope that this is an arrival in Paris which promises something! Down there, victory sword in hand—here it seems to me for a first interview, I have pushed the affair very vigorously, and I saw distinctly in the eye of Milady that it was time for her to begin a retreat. She's locked herself in. It's not your door, Madame, which prevents me from entering, but Lord de Winter would return. My friends are waiting for me at the Pine Cone Inn to celebrate our victory—I don't wish to make them wait.

(Kitty enters softly on the last words of D'Artagnan and sighs.)

KITTY

Oh.

D'ARTAGNAN

What's wrong?

(he turns back)

KITTY

Ah, what a shame.

D'ARTAGNAN

Huh? What shame?

KITTY

Such a handsome boy.

D'ARTAGNAN

Well?

KITTY

Such a handsome face.

D'ARTAGNAN

Is it me you're talking about, my pretty child?

KITTY

Yes.

D'ARTAGNAN

Why are you pitying me?

KITTY

I mean to tell you that you deserve it.

D'ARTAGNAN

Well—speak up—speak up.

KITTY

No—no—leave me.

D'ARTAGNAN

I want you to explain, I want you to say why you pity me—and what I deserve.

KITTY

If Milady heard me, my God—ah, leave me.

D'ARTAGNAN

You are afraid of Milady?

KITTY

Oh!

D'ARTAGNAN

She's bad, isn't she?

KITTY

Shut up—shut up.

D'ARTAGNAN

I won't leave until you have told me—

KITTY

Never.

D'ARTAGNAN

Oh, it's bad.

KITTY

Yet—it would be bad for you to ruin yourself this way.

D'ARTAGNAN

Me—ruin myself?

KITTY

Enough! Enough! I have said too much—Goodbye, Chevalier.

D'ARTAGNAN

Let's see here—a single word.

KITTY

Well, well, try not to love my Milady anymore.

D'ARTAGNAN

(holding her)

But why?

(Someone rings.)

KITTY

Because she will never love you.

D'ARTAGNAN

She won't love me?

KITTY

She's already in love with another—here.

(she shows him a letter)

D'ARTAGNAN

(reading)

"To Baron de Vardes." A rival!

(taking the letter)

KITTY

Ah, my God—give me that letter—give it to me.

D'ARTAGNAN

Adieu, Kitty.

KITTY

My letter.

D'ARTAGNAN

If you want it, come get it at my house.

KITTY

Where's that?

D'ARTAGNAN

Rue des Fossoyeurs, at Mr. Bonacieux's, spice merchant.

CURTAIN

ACT II

Scene 4

D'Artagnan's rooms.

> D'ARTAGNAN

> *(rummaging in the armoire)*

Some empty bottles and some plates. That's what's called a well-kept household—Planchet!

> PLANCHET

> *(entering)*

Sir?

> D'ARTAGNAN

I want lunch.

> PLANCHET

The gentleman wishes lunch?

> D'ARTAGNAN

Yes, what have you to give me?

> PLANCHET

Me? Nothing!

D'ARTAGNAN

What do you mean, nothing? Clown!

PLANCHET

Absolutely nothing.

D'ARTAGNAN

Ah, but do you forget Mr. Planchet that I dined poorly yester-day?

PLANCHET

It's true, the Chevalier dined very poorly.

D'ARTAGNAN

And that I have hardly had lunch?

PLANCHET

The gentleman has hardly had lunch, it's true.

D'ARTAGNAN

And you believe that I will content myself with this treatment?

PLANCHET

It's true that for some time the mess has been sad.

D'ARTAGNAN

Fine—give me my sword.

PLANCHET

(aside)

His sword—what?

D'ARTAGNAN

I am going to lunch with Aramis. I am sure that his lackey is more careful than you, Mr. Planchet. Ah, if I had Bazin in my service instead of having you—

(seeing Planchet who presents him with a letter)

Well—what's this?

PLANCHET

A letter from Mr. Aramis.

D'ARTAGNAN

Ah—ah—what does he say?

(reading)

"My dear Chevalier, my rogue of a librarian, not having brought me yesterday, as he had promised me, the price of my poem and this miserable Bazin, not having been able to promise credit in the quarter, I am going to ask you to dine, this noon. You know how sober I am—a cup of chocolate—some preserves and pastry will suffice. Aramis."

PLANCHET

The fact is one cannot be less exacting.

D'ARTAGNAN

You will tell Aramis that I had gone out when his letter arrived. I am going to lunch with Porthos—what's this again?

PLANCHET

A letter from Mr. Porthos.

D'ARTAGNAN

Give it here.

(reading)

"My dear D'Artagnan, last night in an infamous gambling den I lost a quarter of my salary."

(aside)

What the devil's he going to do there?

(he reads)

"Yesterday, all day, I lived on very hard crusts."

(aside)

So much the better.

(reading)

"I will partake today of your lunch—try to make it copious for I'm hungry."

D'ARTAGNAN

He's absolutely as I am—ah, I have one last resource.

PLANCHET

What, sir?

D'ARTAGNAN

My hat—I have no time to lose.

PLANCHET

To do what?

D'ARTAGNAN

To escape. You will tell Porthos that his letter arrived too late— and that I am dining with Athos.

PLANCHET

(presenting a third letter)

Sir, a letter from Mr. Athos.

D'ARTAGNAN

Perhaps it's an invitation.

(reading)

"My dear Chevalier, I emptied my last bottle of Spanish wine yesterday—"

(speaking)

Truly, Mr. Planchet, I cannot qualify your conduct toward me. Still, Mr. Bonacieux, our landlord has a crowd of good things in his shop—liquors, preserves, little salt foods.

PLANCHET

Yes, sir—but we had promised to pay the first two weeks in advance.

D'ARTAGNAN

And—

PLANCHET

We forgot to do it.

D'ARTAGNAN

(reading)

"But you know I can forego eating."

(speaking)

He's very fortunate.

(reading)

"But not drinking—so bring out your best Madeira, Port or Sherry from your cellar."

(speaking)

I told you to pay your court to that little fruit girl.

PLANCHET

Sir, she gave me my discharge the day before yesterday—and yesterday she replaced me with a lackey of Mr. de la Tremouille.

D'ARTAGNAN

You let yourself be supplanted. Cowardice!

(continuing to read his letter)

"And if your cellar by chance finds itself empty—send to the hotel Pine Cone—that's where one finds the best."

PLANCHET

As if it were the only hotel! But the innkeeper declared he wouldn't furnish anything more except against cash.

D'ARTAGNAN

(looking at Planchet)

Mr. Planchet, I've noticed that in our moments of distress—and these moments occur several times during the month, Mr. Planchet—I've noticed that your temper never suffers any alteration.

PLANCHET

It's true, sir—I've a charming disposition.

D'ARTAGNAN

Mr. Planchet, I've noticed besides that you withstand hunger without your physique suffering.

PLANCHET

It's true. I've a good stomach, sir.

PLANCHET

Mr. Planchet, you have unknown resources.

PLANCHET

Me, sir?

D'ARTAGNAN

Behold, in the very moment I am speaking to you, you are not hungry.

PLANCHET

Oh, sir, if one could speak of it! Here, look at my teeth.

D'ARTAGNAN

(with doubt)

Hum!

PLANCHET

The gentleman is leaving?

D'ARTAGNAN

Yes.

PLANCHET

And if the gentleman's friends come?

D'ARTAGNAN

Have them wait.

PLANCHET

The gentleman has no other orders to give me?

D'ARTAGNAN

(striding toward Planchet)

Only that you carry out carefully all the orders that they give you, dolt, clown, scoundrel!

(He tightens his sword belt and leaves.)

PLANCHET

(alone)

He's hungry! But it's unheard of, these Musketeers, instead of living by order and economy, or of thinking of times of want, in times of abundance—they gamble, they drink, they eat—and when the money is gone—they must tighten their stomachs. I'm not hungry for it. How unjust these masters are! Meaning, on the contrary, I am dying of hunger—I am only waiting for him to leave before eating.

(he pulls from one of his pockets a roast chicken wrapped in paper and from another pocket a bottle of wine)

Ah, here are the only good moments I have in the day.

D'ARTAGNAN

(who made a false show of leaving and who watched Planchet make his arrangements)

Psst!

(Planchet turns frightened.)

D'ARTAGNAN

To your health. Mr. Planchet.

PLANCHET

Ouff!

(he hides his bottle and his roast chicken with his body)

D'ARTAGNAN

Well, but what are you doing there then?

PLANCHET

Sir, I was drinking a glass of water while breaking a crust.

D'ARTAGNAN

A glass of water?

(he takes the glass from the hands of Planchet, watches him, pours some drops of wine on his hand)

PLANCHET

Red water, sir.

D'ARTAGNAN

Mr. Planchet, do you smell poultry?

PLANCHET

It's true—I have a little bite of a turkey thigh.

D'ARTAGNAN

(pulling Planchet, who is obliged to reveal the table)

Ah! Ah! Master Planchet, we are making a banquet or so it appears—there, let's see how the lackey eats the poultry and drinks the wine—while the master is reduced to tightening his belt.

(Planchet separates himself and reaches the door)

Stop and reply.

PLANCHET

Well, the Chevalier has guessed correctly—I have unknown resources.

D'ARTAGNAN

Ah! Ah!

PLANCHET

A private industry.

D'ARTAGNAN

Let's see—your industry, Mr. Planchet—I won't be sorry to
know it.

PLANCHET

The gentleman knows that his chamber is situated just above the
spice store of Mr. Bonacieux?

D'ARTAGNAN

Yes, I know that. Go on.

PLANCHET

Well, I have discovered an ancient Judas.

D'ARTAGNAN

What, an old Judas?

PLANCHET

It seems this chamber belonged to Mr. Bonacieux, and so as to
be able to see from here into his store, he made a trap.

D'ARTAGNAN

Wretch! I hope you haven't been descending by this trap to get
your provisions?

PLANCHET

Fie, sir! Descend, me? That would be stealing. No, sir, it's our
provisions which come up.

D'ARTAGNAN

Ah—they come up?

PLANCHET

Yes, sir.

D'ARTAGNAN

And how do they come up? Explain that to me.

PLANCHET

You want to know it?

D'ARTAGNAN

Yes.

PLANCHET

(opening the Judas)

The gentleman wishes to do me the honor of bending over and
observing?

D'ARTAGNAN

But is there someone in the store?

PLANCHET

Oh! No, sir—at this hour there is never anybody.

D'ARTAGNAN

Oh, I see.

PLANCHET

And see what, sir?

D'ARTAGNAN

I see some bread on a hutch—bottles of liquor and smoked ham.

PLANCHET

Sir, you really see all that?

D'ARTAGNAN

Yes, yes.

PLANCHET

Well, wait a little, sir.

(taking a halberd in a corner)

I am going to have the honor of offering the gentleman a tender bread and a roast leg.

(He pushes the halberd through the Judas.)

D'ARTAGNAN

Oh! Oh! There it is, there it is. The Devil! Could it be that up till now one has been deceived as to the proper use of halberds?

PLANCHET

(who has plucked bread and a leg)

You have seen, sir, the sole manner of their service.

D'ARTAGNAN

Good! Here's the bread and the leg of lamb—but the wine, sir, the wine!

PLANCHET

Sir, chance has caused me to know well a Spaniard who voyaged in the new world.

D'ARTAGNAN

What connection can the new world have with the wine that you drank to your health when I entered Mr. Planchet?

PLANCHET

In Mexico the natives of the country hunt the tiger and the bull with simple flowing knots that they cast over the throats of those terrible animals.

D'ARTAGNAN

Mr. Planchet, I don't see at present—.

PLANCHET

The gentleman is going to see. At first, I couldn't believe that one could arrive at that degree of dexterity to throw at twenty or thirty feet a rope when one wished, but as my friend placed a bottle at thirty feet and each time took the neck in the knot, I worked at this trick and today I can throw a lasso almost as well as a man from the new world. Would the Chevalier like to judge?

(Drawing a rope from his pocket.)

D'ARTAGNAN

Why yes, I would be curious to be present at this exercise.

PLANCHET

Well—

(throwing the rope)

Here—

(a bottle comes up taken by the neck)

D'ARTAGNAN

But that's liquor and not wine.

PLANCHET

Chevalier, with a bottle of liquor which I will sell for two pounds, I will buy four bottles of burgundy at ten sous a piece. Now, sir, permit me to offer you the roast.

(he goes to take a line)

D'ARTAGNAN

You mean to say the fried food?

PLANCHET

No, sir, the roast.

D'ARTAGNAN

The fried food.

PLANCHET

If the Chevalier's window gave on a pond, on a lake, on a river, I would fish carp and trout *en brochette*. But the window gives on a chicken coop, I fish chicken. The Chevalier is going to see how this works.

(he throws his line and brings back a chicken)

One need only take time to throw out the line. There—

D'ARTAGNAN

Mr. Planchet, you are a comedian!

PLANCHET

Sir!

D'ARTAGNAN

But seeing the urgency of the situation, I pardon you. Go pluck this chicken and roast him. Hold—one knocks—it's probably our friends.

PLANCHET

Yes, it's probably them.

D'ARTAGNAN

(aside)

This humorist is full of ingenious inventions. He's a treasure without parallel among lackeys.

PLANCHET

(recoiling, very upset)

Sir, sir.

D'ARTAGNAN

Well, what's wrong?

PLANCHET

Mr. Bonacieux, our landlord.

D'ARTAGNAN

Oh! Oh! Were you seen throwing a lasso or fishing with the rope?

PLANCHET

I don't know, sir, but at all hazards, stuff this chicken in my pocket.

BONACIEUX

(in the antechamber)

Hum! Hum!

D'ARTAGNAN

My word, so much the worse—let whatever happens, happen. Enter Mr. Bonacieux—enter.

(Bonacieux enters—Planchet leaves, furtively.)

BONACIEUX

Mr. Chevalier, I am indeed your servant.

D'ARTAGNAN

It is I who am yours, sir. Planchet—an armchair—well—where is he now? Excuse me, sir—I am served by a clown who deserves the galley.

(He brings an armchair.)

BONACIEUX

Don't trouble yourself, sir—I have heard you spoken of as a Chevalier both very honest and brave.

D'ARTAGNAN

Sir—

BONACIEUX

And it is this last quality which has decided me to address you.

D'ARTAGNAN

To do what?

BONACIEUX

To confide a secret to you.

D'ARTAGNAN

A secret? Speak, sir, speak.

BONACIEUX

It's about my wife.

D'ARTAGNAN

You have a wife?

BONACIEUX

Who is linen maid to the Queen, yes, sir—and who neither lacks youth nor beauty. They made me marry her almost three years ago, even though she had almost nothing—because Mr. de la Porte, the tailor to the Queen, is her god father and protects her.

D'ARTAGNAN

Well, sir?

BONACIEUX

Well, sir, my wife was kidnapped yesterday as she left her work room.

D'ARTAGNAN

She, your wife, has been kidnapped? And by whom?

BONACIEUX

I cannot say for sure, sir, but in any case, I am convinced there is less in this kidnapping of love than of politics.

D'ARTAGNAN

Less of love than politics—but what do you suspect?

BONACIEUX

I don't know if I ought to tell you what I suspect.

D'ARTAGNAN

Sir, I will observe that I've asked you nothing; it is you who have come; it is you who have told me you have a secret to confide—do so in your humor.

(rising)

It is time for you to retire, again.

BONACIEUX

No, sir, I have confidence in you—I believe then that it isn't because of her love affairs that my wife has been arrested.

D'ARTAGNAN

So much the worse for you.

BONACIEUX

But because of a much greater lady than she—

D'ARTAGNAN

Ah, bah! Would it be because of the loves affairs of Miss de Combalet?

BONACIEUX

Much higher, sir, much higher.

D'ARTAGNAN

Of Madame de Chevreuse?

BONACIEUX

Much higher—sir, very much higher.

D'ARTAGNAN

Of the—?

BONACIEUX

Yes, sir.

D'ARTAGNAN

And with whom?

BONACIEUX

With whom if not the Duke of Buck—?

D'ARTAGNAN

With the Duke of—?

BONACIEUX

Exactly.

D'ARTAGNAN

But how do you of all people know this?

BONACIEUX

Ah—how do I know it?—well—

D'ARTAGNAN

No half confidences—

(rising)

—or you understand.

BONACIEUX

I know it from my wife, sir—from my wife herself.

D'ARTAGNAN

How's that?

BONACIEUX

My wife came four days ago; she confided to me that the Queen, at that moment was in great fear for the Queen believed—

D'ARTAGNAN

What did the Queen believe?

BONACIEUX

She believed that someone had written to the Duke of Buckingham in her name.

D'ARTAGNAN

Bah!

BONACIEUX

Yes, to make him come to Paris—and once in Paris, to snare him in some trap.

D'ARTAGNAN

But what has your wife to do with all this?

BONACIEUX

They know her devotion to the Queen and wanted to separate her from her mistress to get Her Majesty's secrets or to seduce her to serve her like a spy.

D'ARTAGNAN

That's likely, but the man who kidnapped her—do you know him?

BONACIEUX

I don't know his name—but my wife pointed him out to me one day—he's a lord of haughty name—white teeth—a scar on his temple.

D'ARTAGNAN

But that's my man!

BONACIEUX

Your man?

D'ARTAGNAN

Yes, probably, and if he is my man—I will have a double vengeance—but where to meet this fellow?

BONACIEUX

I don't know.

D'ARTAGNAN

You have no other information?

BONACIEUX

In fact, only this letter.

D'ARTAGNAN

Give me.

(reading)

"Don't look for your wife—she will be returned to you when there's no further need for her—if you take a single step to find her, you are lost." Well—it's positive but, after all, it's only a threat.

BONACIEUX

Yes, sir, but this threat frightens me; I am not a swordsman—and I'm afraid of the Bastille.

D'ARTAGNAN

Hum! I don't care for the Bastille myself—but still, it's only a question of a sword fight.

BONACIEUX

Now, sir, I had counted much on you in this matter?

D'ARTAGNAN

True?

BONACIEUX

Seeing you ceaselessly surrounded by Musketeers with a very proud air, and noticing that these Musketeers were those of Mr. de Treville and consequently enemies of the Cardinal, I had thought that you and your friends all in rendering service to our poor Queen, would be enchanted to play a trick on the Cardinal.

D'ARTAGNAN

It's indeed tempting, I know it.

BONACIEUX

And then I thought again—that—since you live with me—distracted no doubt by your great preoccupations you had forgotten to pay my rent.

D'ARTAGNAN

Ah! There we are—

BONACIEUX

A delay for which I have never bothered you a single instant—I had thought that you would have respect for my delicacy.

D'ARTAGNAN

Why indeed, dear sir, believe that I am full of gratitude for such a procedure.

BONACIEUX

Counting, moreover that you did me the honor of living in my hotel, never speaking to you of your future rent—

(D'Artagnan gestures.)

And adding that counting still, if against all probability, you were inconvenienced at the moment, to offer you fifty pistoles.

D'ARTAGNAN

Oh, never, sir, I could not accept—

(Bonacieux forces money into his pocket.)

D'ARTAGNAN

But to make me such an offer you must be rich?

BONACIEUX

Without being rich, I am at my ease. I have amassed two or three hundred thousand shillings of rent.

D'ARTAGNAN

Dear Mr. Bonacieux, I am totally at your service.

BONACIEUX

I believe someone is knocking on your door, Mr. Chevalier.

D'ARTAGNAN

Oh, by God, you fall in marvelously—my friends are coming to ask dinner of me—your business will be deliberated in council.

BONACIEUX

(to Planchet who is entering)

My dear Mr. Planchet, follow your master in his good disposition towards me, and we shall see things, Mr. Planchet, such things. That's all I can tell you. Gentlemen, your humble servant.

(Enter Porthos.)

D'ARTAGNAN

My dear Mr. Porthos, I present to you the pearl of Landlords—Mr. Porthos, one of my best friends.

PORTHOS

(low)

He really looks bad, your landlord.

D'ARTAGNAN

(aside)

For a spice merchant, I don't find it so.

BONACIEUX

Sir, I don't need to tell you that my entire house is at your service.

(Bonacieux exits.)

PORTHOS

Mousqueton, take my cloak.

D'ARTAGNAN

(returning after having accompanied Bonacieux)

Ah! Ah! Your cold hasn't gotten worse, Porthos?

PORTHOS

Where were you then yesterday evening when we were looking all over for you? Here—at the Cabaret and at Mr. Treville's—without finding you?

ARAMIS

(entering and having heard Porthos' question)

Porthos, my friend, you are of an incredible indiscretion. Where was he? At his affairs, without doubt—when you head down the Rue aux Ours, would you like to have Mousqueton ask where you were going?

PORTHOS

Rue aux Ours—when I go to the Rue aux Ours.

ARAMIS

You go where you wish and it's nobody's business.

(to Athos who comes in)

Right, Athos?

ATHOS

So long, at least, as he hasn't discovered a cellar full of everything—in which case it would be a crime not to give shares to his
friends. Have we wine, Planchet?

PLANCHET

Yes, sir—and worthy of you, I hope.

ATHOS

Then all goes well.

PORTHOS

You really love wine, Athos.

ATHOS

It's not wine I love, it's drunkenness.

D'ARTAGNAN

I don't understand—to dinner.

ATHOS

Grimaud, I give you leave.

PORTHOS

Go, Mousqueton.

ARAMIS

Leave, Bazin.

D'ARTAGNAN

Now, let's talk.

ATHOS

That's to say—let's drink, you mean.

D'ARTAGNAN

Planchet, go down to my landlord, Mr. Bonacieux and beg him to send us five or six bottles of foreign wine, and particularly Spanish wine.

PORTHOS

Ah, so! You then have open credit with your landlord?

D'ARTAGNAN

Yes, counting from today—and be easy—if the wine is bad, we will see about fetching more.

ARAMIS

It must be used not abused, D'Artagnan.

ATHOS

I've always said that D'Artagnan had the best head of the four of us.

PORTHOS

But now, what's wrong?

D'ARTAGNAN

It's that Buckingham has come to Paris on a false letter from the Queen; that the Cardinal is by way of playing a bad role toward Her Majesty and that the wife of our landlord, god-daughter of Mr. de la Porte and confidante of the Queen, has been kidnapped.

ATHOS

Well?

D'ARTAGNAN

Well, Mr. Bonacieux wishes to get his wife back.

ATHOS

The fool!

ARAMIS

To me it seems the business isn't so bad—and that one can extract from this brave man a hundred pistoles.

PORTHOS

A hundred pistoles! That's a pretty job—zounds!

ATHOS

Yes, now it's a question of knowing if a hundred pistoles is worth the trouble of risking our four heads.

D'ARTAGNAN

Hush!

PORTHOS

What?

ARAMIS

Silence!

BONACIEUX

(on the stairs)

Gentlemen! Gentlemen!

D'ARTAGNAN

Eh! It's my worthy landlord.

BONACIEUX

(entering)

Help me! Help! Help!

(All rise, except Athos.)

PORTHOS

What's wrong?

BONACIEUX

Gentlemen, they're going to arrest me—four men—down there. Save me! Save me!

PORTHOS

Zounds! Arrest a landlord who has such good wine!

D'ARTAGNAN

A moment gentlemen—it's not courage we lack here, it's prudence.

PORTHOS

Now we are not going to let this brave man be arrested.

ATHOS

You will let D'Artagnan decide, Porthos.

(D'Artagnan causes the guards who have come to arrest Bonacieux to enter.)

D'ARTAGNAN

Come in, gentlemen, come in, you are here in my home, that is to say, in the home of a faithful servant of the King and the Cardinal.

ADJUTANT

Then gentlemen, you will not oppose us in executing the order we have received.

D'ARTAGNAN

Quite the contrary and we will support you strongly if there is need.

PORTHOS

But what's he saying?

ATHOS

You are naive, Porthos, shut up.

BONACIEUX

(low to D'Artagnan)

But you just promised me....

D'ARTAGNAN

Silence—we cannot save you and remain free—if we make a move to protect you they will arrest us with you.

BONACIEUX

But it seems to me that after—

D'ARTAGNAN

Gentlemen, I have no motive to protect the man you claim. I have seen him today for the first time and even on that occasion—he will tell you himself, he came to touch on my rent— Isn't that true, Mr. Bonacieux—reply.

(low)

Answer.

BONACIEUX

Yes, gentlemen—it's the pure truth—but, sir, didn't you say—

D'ARTAGNAN

(low)

Silence! Silence about me and my friends! Silence above all about the Queen or you will ruin everybody without saving yourself.

(aloud)

Well—what do you say? Speak up. You offered me some money—you wish to corrupt me—me to protect you? Me to oppose the execution of His Eminence's orders. You are still a strange rogue! Try corruption on Her Majesty's guards. Oh, take him gentlemen—take him—for in truth, he's a man who is losing his head.

ADJUTANT

Come, come, friend, come with us and no resistance.

D'ARTAGNAN

Mr. Adjutant, can I drink your health and you drink mine?

(He fills two glasses.)

ADJUTANT

It will be an honor for me, Mr. Guardsman.

D'ARTAGNAN

Then to your Master, sir.

ADJUTANT

And to yours and those of your friends.

D'ARTAGNAN

And above all to the King and the Cardinal.

BONACIEUX

When one thinks this is with my wine!

ADJUTANT

Come on, forward, march.

(returning)

Gentlemen, your very humble servant.

(The guards leave taking Bonacieux.)

PORTHOS

Why, what devilish species of villainy have you committed then, D'Artagnan! Fie! Four Musketeers to let an unfortunate who cries for help in their midst be arrested! A gentleman drink with a bailiff! I'm lost, my word of honor. What? You approve of what he's just done?

ATHOS

I trust him very much. Not only do I approve of you, D'Artagnan—I congratulate you again.

D'ARTAGNAN

And now, gentlemen, we are hurled into an adventure in which we are either ruined or we'll make our fortune—more than ever let us swear fidelity to our motto: "All for one—one for all."

PORTHOS

Now, I wish I understood more clearly.

ATHOS

It's useless.

ARAMIS

Watch—extend hands and swear, Porthos.

D'ARTAGNAN

All for one.

ALL TOGETHER

One for all.

D'ARTAGNAN

Now, gentlemen—you know it—complete freedom.

PORTHOS

I have a rendezvous with a certain great lady—Planchet, adjust my collar—my cloak.

ARAMIS

Me, I have some business with a celebrated theologian.

PORTHOS

And you, Athos?

ATHOS

Me—as I am occupied neither with love nor with women—I will remain.

ARAMIS and PORTHOS

(to D'Artagnan & Athos)

Well—au revoir.

D'ARTAGNAN and ATHOS

Au revoir.

(Aramis & Porthos exit.)

D'ARTAGNAN

Bravo! Remain Athos—besides—there's still some wine in the bottles and it would be ungrateful of you to leave.

ATHOS

Come on, D'Artagnan—face me—at least like Aramis haven't you some thesis to sustain or like Porthos some great lady to walk with?

D'ARTAGNAN

(sadly)

Ah—my dear Athos—!

ATHOS

A sigh—drink, D'Artagnan, and take care of those sighs.

D'ARTAGNAN

Then what?

ATHOS

D'Artagnan, be careful.

(he drinks)

D'ARTAGNAN

You were saying?

ATHOS

I say you are amorous—

D'ARTAGNAN

Imagine a woman.

ATHOS

An angel—right.

D'ARTAGNAN

No—a demon.

ATHOS

She's less to be feared.

D'ARTAGNAN

Oh, but it's useless.

ATHOS

What's useless?

D'ARTAGNAN

I wanted to ask your advice.

ATHOS

Well?

D'ARTAGNAN

It's already too late.

ATHOS

Because you believe that I am drunk, D'Artagnan—but I never have clearer ideas than when I'm in my cups. Speak then, I'm all ears.

D'ARTAGNAN

No, it's not because you are drunk, my dear Athos, it's because, having never loved—

ATHOS

Ah, that's true, I've never loved.

(he drinks)

D'ARTAGNAN

You see—heart of stone.

ATHOS

Tender heart, broken heart.

D'ARTAGNAN

What are you saying?

ATHOS

I say that love is a lottery where one wins—wins—death—have you won or lost, D'Artagnan?

D'ARTAGNAN

I believe I have lost.

ATHOS

Then you are indeed happy—believe me, D'Artagnan—always lose.

D'ARTAGNAN

For a moment, I believed that she loved me.

ATHOS

And she loves another, right? Remember this well—there's not a man who didn't believe himself loved by his mistress who wasn't deceived by his mistress.

D'ARTAGNAN

Oh—she wasn't my mistress.

ATHOS

She wasn't your mistress and you complain—she wasn't your wife and you complain—let's drink.

D'ARTAGNAN

But then, philosopher that you are—instruct me, help me—I need to know and be consoled.

ATHOS

Consoled about what?

D'ARTAGNAN

About my misfortune—by God—I loved and she didn't love me.

ATHOS

Your misfortune is laughable—D'Artagnan and I am curious to know what you would say if I told you a love story.

D'ARTAGNAN

That happened to you?

ATHOS

Or to one of my friends—what does it matter!

D'ARTAGNAN

Speak, Athos, speak.

ATHOS

Drink up and we'll be better.

D'ARTAGNAN

Drink up and speak up.

ATHOS

In fact, both of these things go marvelously well together. One of my friends—one of my friends, you hear—not me—but a Count from my province—that is to say a Count de Berry—noble like a Rohan or a Montmorency, became amorous at twenty-five years of age of a pretty girl of sixteen—pretty as love itself—she didn't please—she intoxicated.

D'ARTAGNAN

She's like her!

ATHOS

Ah, there you go interrupting. She lived in an isolated house—between the village and the Château—with her brother who was a Curé, both were strangers. They came from no one knew where but in seeing her so beautiful and the brother so pious, no one thought to ask them where they came from. As for the rest, they were said to be of good birth. One day, the brother disappeared or pretended to disappear. My friend, who was the lord of the county, could have seduced her or taken her by force. Who would have come to the aid of a young girl—ignorant—unknown? Unfortunately, he was an honest man, he married her—the fool—the stupid idiot—the imbecile.

D'ARTAGNAN

Since he loved her, it seems to me—

ATHOS

Pay attention. Six months later, at the death of his father—he brought her to the Château—and made her the first lady of the province—to do her justice, she held the rank perfectly. Drink up!

D'ARTAGNAN

Well—

ATHOS

Well, one day she went on a hunt with her husband. She fell from her horse and fainted—the Count hurled himself to her aid and she was suffocating in her clothes. He cut them away with his dagger and exposed her shoulder—

(laughing loudly)

Guess what he had on her shoulder, D'Artagnan?

D'ARTAGNAN

How the devil should I know?

ATHOS

A fleur de lys! The angel was a demon; the poor girl had stolen sacred vessels from a church.

D'ARTAGNAN

Horrible! And what did your friend do?

ATHOS

The Count was a great lord. He had over his lands the right of justice high and low—he finished by tearing the clothes from the Countess, he tied her hands behind her back and hung her from a tree.

D'ARTAGNAN

Heavens! A murder, Athos?

ATHOS

Not much better—but we need some wine, it seems to me.

D'ARTAGNAN

No—there's still a full bottle.

ATHOS

Fie! That cured me of beautiful women, poetic and amorous. God grant you as much.

D'ARTAGNAN

Then it was you?

ATHOS

Did I say it was me? Then to the devil, the secret!

D'ARTAGNAN

And she is dead?

ATHOS

By God.

D'ARTAGNAN

And her brother?

ATHOS

Her brother, I tried to learn his whereabouts to hang in his turn, but one could never find him. He was without doubt the first lover and accomplice of the beauty—a worthy man who pretended to be a cure so as to marry his mistress and give her a chance. He will have been quartered, I hope.

D'ARTAGNAN

(falling on the table)

Oh! My love! My God!

ATHOS

(looking at D'Artagnan)

Some wine, Planchet. Ah, men no longer know how to drink, and yet this one is one of the best.

(Planchet enters with two bottles of wine.)

CURTAIN

ACT II

Scene 5

The interior of Mr. Bonacieux's shop—four men in black and an Adjutant talking. Everything is topsy in the house.

ADJUTANT

(reading)

"And search made in the entire house, we declare that we found no paper except as those attached in file 'C'. In Testimony of which we have signed."

(he signs)

ONE OF THE MEN IN BLACK

Is that all?

ADJUTANT

Relative to the writings, yes. Now it's a question of proceeding to the true object of our mission.

ANOTHER MAN IN BLACK

(rising before the table)

What is that?

ADJUTANT

Here it is—as the aforesaid Bonacieux can and must have accomplices—and that it is nine o'clock past noon. Which means
nightfall and that it is especially at night, when accomplices
meet—the object of our mission is to stay in the house perma-
nently of the aforesaid Bonacieux and to let enter all those who
knock and not to let anyone leave until after confrontation and
interrogation.

ONE OF THE MEN IN BLACK

And women are involved in it?

ADJUTANT

Women especially, considering the great malefactor in all this is
the wife, not the husband.

SECOND BLACK MAN

It seems to me someone's knocking on the door.

ADJUTANT

Lights out—and each to his post.

(They extinguish the lamp—complete obscurity.)

MADAME BONACIEUX

(after having knocked outside softly, pushes open the door)

Really, this is singular—the door open and no one in the house.

ADJUTANT

Psst!

*(One of the men glides behind Madame Bonacieux and
goes to close the door.)*

MADAME BONACIEUX

Well! I think I heard—Mr. Bonacieux—Mr. Bonacieux.

(she turns around. The adjutant is hidden in the corner)

He must have left. Let's light things up—happily there's some fire.

(She lights a candle at the fireplace and perceives the Adjutant.)

MADAME BONACIEUX

Who are you? What do you want with me?

ADJUTANT

Silence.

MADAME BONACIEUX

What are you doing here? Help—help!

ADJUTANT

To me, my friends! I believe we hold the one the world is looking for.

MADAME BONACIEUX

What do you want of me? I am the mistress of this house.

ADJUTANT

Exactly.

MADAME BONACIEUX

I am Madame Bonacieux.

ADJUTANT

Marvelous.

MADAME BONACIEUX

Pardon, gentlemen. Help! Help! Ah!

(At this moment, the trap door opens and the audience sees D'Artagnan descend—legs first, then the body, then the head.)

D'ARTAGNAN

Hold tight! Here I am!

PLANCHET

(in the room)

But you are going to get killed.

D'ARTAGNAN

Shut up—imbecile.

(D'Artagnan jumps into the middle of the room.)

ADJUTANT

What's this?

D'ARTAGNAN

What's this? I am going to tell you. It's a gentleman who does not permit a woman to be mistreated in front of him. Come, come, release this woman.

ADJUTANT

Sir, this is in the name of the king.

D'ARTAGNAN

Release this woman.

ADJUTANT

(to his men)

Grab her—take her!

(He pulls out his sword.)

D'ARTAGNAN

Ah—swords, is it? So much the better. I'm better with a sword than a stick. Gentlemen, watch your feathers.

(Tumultuous combat. The five men end by taking flight. Some by the windows, others by the doors—D'Artagnan closes the door behind them and returns to Madame Bonacieux.)

D'ARTAGNAN

Come, come, Madame, rest assured—my God—! What, has she fainted? It's nothing—they are gone, Madame. The Devil take me—she is charming!

MADAME BONACIEUX

Ah!

D'ARTAGNAN

Really, that made her come to.

MADAME BONACIEUX

Ah, sir, it's you who saved me—permit me to thank you. Oh! Pardon me, I will try to prove to you that I am not an ingrate. But, tell me what these men wished from me, who I took at first for thieves and why isn't Mr. Bonacieux here—?

D'ARTAGNAN

Those men were agents of the Cardinal. As for Mr. Bonacieux, he's in the Bastille.

MADAME BONACIEUX

My husband is in the Bastille? Oh, my God, poor dear man—poor innocent man—what has he done?

D'ARTAGNAN

His greatest crime, Madame, is, I believe to have the fortune and misfortune to be your husband.

MADAME BONACIEUX

But sir, you know then—

D'ARTAGNAN

I know you were kidnapped, Madame.

MADAME BONACIEUX

And by whom? Do you know?

D'ARTAGNAN

Wasn't it a man of between forty and forty-five years of age—black hair—with a scar on his left temple?

MADAME BONACIEUX

Hush—don't say his name.

D'ARTAGNAN

I don't have to avoid it, I don't know it—you might know it perchance?

MADAME BONACIEUX

Silence!

D'ARTAGNAN

But then?

MADAME BONACIEUX

Silence, in heaven's name! But tell me—has Mr. Bonacieux figured out why I was kidnapped?

D'ARTAGNAN

He attributed it to a political motive.

MADAME BONACIEUX

Then he didn't suspect me for a single instant?

D'ARTAGNAN

Oh—far from it, Madame! He was very proud of your wisdom and especially of your love. But how did you escape—you—a prisoner?

MADAME BONACIEUX

I profited from a moment when I was left alone and I got out the window with the aid of my bed sheets.

D'ARTAGNAN

But you risked your life?

MADAME BONACIEUX

Would I had ten lives that I might risk them.

D'ARTAGNAN

Why have you risked coming here now you're free?

MADAME BONACIEUX

According to all probability, they won't know I've flown the coop until tomorrow.

D'ARTAGNAN

Ah! That's true.

MADAME BONACIEUX

And it was important that I see my husband this evening.

D'ARTAGNAN

To place yourself under his protection?

MADAME BONACIEUX

Oh, poor man! You have seen he is incapable of protecting me. No—but he could serve me in another way.

D'ARTAGNAN

In what way?

MADAME BONACIEUX

Oh, it's not my secret and I cannot tell you.

D'ARTAGNAN

But what must your husband do?

MADAME BONACIEUX

(getting ready to leave)

I will do it myself.

D'ARTAGNAN

You are leaving here?

MADAME BONACIEUX

It must be done.

D'ARTAGNAN

And you go alone in the streets! And the thieves?

MADAME BONACIEUX

I haven't a penny on me.

D'ARTAGNAN

You forget this pretty blazoned handkerchief, which has fallen at your feet and which I put back in your pocket.

MADAME BONACIEUX

Be quiet! Be quiet! Do you want me to be lost?

D'ARTAGNAN

You see indeed there is still some danger for you since a single word makes you tremble. Hold on—cast away all fear—rely on me—Read in my eyes all there is of devotion and in my heart all there is of sympathy.

MADAME BONACIEUX

Oh, I would indeed be ungrateful if I doubted you—after the service you have rendered me. Ask my secrets, I will tell you them—but those of others—never.

D'ARTAGNAN

Well, so be it! Free for you to try to hide them from me; but free for me to try and discover them.

MADAME BONACIEUX

Oh, by the gratitude that I owe you, protect yourself well, sir! Don't mix with anything regarding me; don't try to aid me in what I accomplish—I ask you in the name of the interest I inspired in you—in the name of the service you have rendered me and which I will never forget in my life. No, no, believe what I tell you—don't bother with me—Let me not exist any more for you—let it be as if you had never seen me.

D'ARTAGNAN

But is there such danger?

MADAME BONACIEUX

Yes, there is danger of prison; there is danger to life in knowing me.

D'ARTAGNAN

Then I will never leave you.

MADAME BONACIEUX

Sir, in the name of heaven, in the name of military honor—in the name of the courtesy of a gentleman, leave me. There—it's 10:30—at the house, they expect me or rather, I am already a half hour late.

D'ARTAGNAN

Madame, I don't know how to resist when you ask me this way. Be free—I will retire.

MADAME BONACIEUX

No—let me leave. You leave later—and your oath?

D'ARTAGNAN

Well?

MADAME BONACIEUX

That you won't spy on me—that you won't follow me.

D'ARTAGNAN

Word of a gentleman, Madame.

MADAME BONACIEUX

Ah, I know quite well you have a brave heart.

(giving him her hand)

D'ARTAGNAN

(kissing her hand)

When will I see you again?

MADAME BONACIEUX

You want to see me again?

D'ARTAGNAN

Oh, very much.

MADAME BONACIEUX

Well—leave it to me.

D'ARTAGNAN

I count on your word.

MADAME BONACIEUX

Count on it.

(She exits.)

D'ARTAGNAN

Well, I declare that whoever sees clearly in all this that's happening has sharp eyes—Aramis, Madame Boistracy, the Queen, the Duke of Buckingham—the Cardinal, Madame Bonacieux. How the devil do all these people find themselves mixed together? She's charming, this petite little Madame Bonacieux—an air of a Princess—a heart, courage, wit—and wife of that frightful merchant. In fact, you must come to Paris to see this—it never happens at Tarbes like this.

PLANCHET

(across the ceiling)

Sir, sir, are you still there?

D'ARTAGNAN

Yes.

PLANCHET

Sir, they're knocking at the door.

D'ARTAGNAN

Who?

PLANCHET

I think it's the guard.

D'ARTAGNAN

Bah!

PLANCHET

I hear the butts of muskets. Shall I open?

D'ARTAGNAN

Without doubt, since I am not there.

PLANCHET

Fine. Don't budge.

(The trap door closes.)

D'ARTAGNAN

Ah, throw me my cloak and my hat! Plague! There's no danger for me to budge. Only it seems to me that as additional precaution, I ought to close the door.

(he goes to the door at back after having stifled the candle, but as he approaches, the door opens and Milady, dressed exactly as Madame Bonacieux appears)

Oh! Oh! What do I see?

MILADY

Isn't this the place and am I mistaken? Now—here's the boutique, then the area behind the shop—I am indeed at the home of Mr. Bonacieux, spice merchant—I saw the name above the door.

(going to the window)

Count! Count!

(Rochefort appears.)

(D'Artagnan in the boutique stumbles against a cask.)

MILADY

(closing the window)

I am deceived—there is someone.

D'ARTAGNAN

Already returned?

MILADY

Returned and from where?

D'ARTAGNAN

It's not her voice.

MILADY

Who are you?

D'ARTAGNAN

But I ask you the same question, Madame—only if you refuse to reply—

(going to the chimney and lighting a candle)

ROCHEFORT

(at the window)

Do you have need of me?

MILADY

I don't know—but hold yourself in readiness—

(recognizing D'Artagnan)

My Gascon!

(to Rochefort)

Don't worry about a thing.

D'ARTAGNAN

Milady.

MILADY

Well, they didn't deceive me?

D'ARTAGNAN

They didn't deceive you, Madame—and what did they tell you?

MILADY

They told me that a certain Chevalier D'Artagnan, who paid court to Milady de Winter, was at the same time amorous of a little shop girl named Madame Bonacieux.

D'ARTAGNAN

Me—amorous, Milady? I only saw her this evening for the first time.

MILADY

You saw her this evening?

D'ARTAGNAN

Oh—'S'death, what have I said?

MILADY

I thought she was in a secure place.

D'ARTAGNAN

(aside)

She knows about her arrest.

(aloud)

That is to say—no—Madame—and I am going to be frank—I knew her for a long while and she is from my country, and this evening, seeing that after three days she hadn't returned, I came down to ask Mr. Bonacieux news about her, and having found the house empty, I was here—I waited, I found it singular—now you are come and I am happy.

MILADY

You found the house empty?

D'ARTAGNAN

Damnation—look!

MILADY

What do you mean to say about it?

D'ARTAGNAN

And as I told you, Madame, I am happy—very happy.

MILADY

Fine, Chevalier, I know what I wanted to know.

D'ARTAGNAN

And what did you want to know?

MILADY

I wanted to know how far to rely on the oaths of love of the Chevalier D'Artagnan.

D'ARTAGNAN

Madame, in the name of heaven.

MILADY

I hope you will have the grace to believe that Milady de Winter has too much self-respect to enter into a competition with Madame Bonacieux. Await her return, Chevalier—ah—I don't need to tell you that it will be useless for you to present yourself henceforth at the Hotel at the Place Royale.

D'ARTAGNAN

Madame—listen to me, please—

(He bars her passage.)

MILADY

Oh! I hope that entering here freely, I will leave freely.

ROCHEFORT

(opening the window)

Milady! Milady!

D'ARTAGNAN

(turning)

My man from Meung! Ah, this time you won't escape me, I hope.

(he jumps out the window and one hears his voice in the distance)

Ah—coward! Ah—wretch—ah—false gentleman!

ROCHEFORT

(returning and striding over the window)

He recognized you?

MILADY

Yes, but I have given a reason for my presence.

ROCHEFORT

There's no fear that he will question the motive that brings us here?

MILADY

Not the least. And you?

ROCHEFORT

Didn't you see? He jumped over my head—and he's capable of running all the way to the river—he's enraged.

MILADY

But—

ROCHEFORT

But—let's get out of here. It seems the blow is misdirected—right?

MILADY

There is still this damned Gascon who's mixing in our affairs.

ROCHEFORT

Be easy, he will pay for everything! Come! Come!

(At the moment they leave the back room, one sees the legs of Planchet appear.)

PLANCHET

(while crossing the ceiling)

Mr. D'Artagnan! Mr. D'Artagnan, where are you, Mr. D'Artagnan? Ah, my God! My God! May he not have gone to deliver himself up.

D'ARTAGNAN

(reentering)

You haven't seen him?

PLANCHET

Yes, sir?

D'ARTAGNAN

Him, this demon incarnate who appears to me without cease and whom I can never meet.

PLANCHET

Listen to me. The guard came. They found Mr. Athos who was in your room and carried him off.

D'ARTAGNAN

Horrors—and he let them do it?

PLANCHET

They took him for you.

D'ARTAGNAN

And he didn't explain?

PLANCHET

Much to the contrary—I was going to speak—but he put his finger on his mouth—then I understood.

D'ARTAGNAN

O brave Athos! I recognize you well in that.

(The back door opens. Enter Madame Bonacieux.)

MADAME BONACIEUX

Chevalier! Chevalier! Are you still here?

D'ARTAGNAN

Madame Bonacieux!

MADAME BONACIEUX

Yes.

D'ARTAGNAN

My God—what's wrong with you? Planchet! Planchet!

MADAME BONACIEUX

No, no—don't bother about me.

D'ARTAGNAN

What has happened?

MADAME BONACIEUX

I lost a half hour.

D'ARTAGNAN

Well?

MADAME BONACIEUX

I got there too late. A woman dressed like me with a similar handkerchief to this presented herself at the house on the Rue Vaugirard and gave him the address.

D'ARTAGNAN

A woman dressed like you—she came from here.

MADAME BONACIEUX

Did you see her? You have spoken to her?

D'ARTAGNAN

Yes.

MADAME BONACIEUX

What became of her?

D'ARTAGNAN

A demon I've pursued for three weeks and that I will pursue all my life, if necessary, appeared at this window. I ran after him. During this time, I don't know what became of her. And wait, this man—it's the same man who kidnapped you.

MADAME BONACIEUX

My God!

D'ARTAGNAN

And additionally, they came to arrest me.

MADAME BONACIEUX

Where?

D'ARTAGNAN

Upstairs where I live.

MADAME BONACIEUX

They didn't find you?

D'ARTAGNAN

No, but they found one of my friends, who let himself be taken in my place.

MADAME BONACIEUX

So that they think they've got you?

D'ARTAGNAN

Exactly.

MADAME BONACIEUX

Mr. D'Artagnan—there's not a moment to lose.

D'ARTAGNAN

Give your orders!

MADAME BONACIEUX

Tell your lackey to explore the neighborhood.

D'ARTAGNAN

Planchet—you understand.

PLANCHET

I am running, sir.

MADAME BONACIEUX

You are going to accompany me?

D'ARTAGNAN

Where to?

MADAME BONACIEUX

To the place he's hiding. My God! My God! Let us arrive in time.

D'ARTAGNAN

Let's hurry.

PLANCHET

(at the back door)

One cannot come in. When one says you can't come in.

(Enter a man wrapped in his cloak.)

MAN

Yes, but I am coming in.

(He pushes Planchet and enters.)

PLANCHET

Sir, sir—help!

D'ARTAGNAN

Ah—here's somebody who's going to pay the score for all.

MAN

Dare you indeed, comedian?

D'ARTAGNAN

(drawing his sword)

You were told you couldn't come in, sir.

MAN

And I replied by coming in.

D'ARTAGNAN

Who are you?

MAN

And who are you?

D'ARTAGNAN

Oh—'S'death, you're going to find out.

MAN

You think so?

(casting off his cloak)

MADAME BONACIEUX

Fine.

(she puts herself between them and seizes the swords)

Milord! Milord!

D'ARTAGNAN

(taking three steps back)

Sir—you must be?

MADAME BONACIEUX

Milord, Duke of Buckingham.

(to D'Artagnan)

And now, you can destroy us all.

D'ARTAGNAN

You here, Milord?

(to Madame Bonacieux)

What's he doing here?

MADAME BONACIEUX

Oh—I don't know—it is only my Lord who can tell you.

BUCKINGHAM

It's very simple. On presenting myself at the Rue de la Harpe, they showed me the handkerchief and told me I was expected at Rue de Fossoyeurs, near the Luxembourg—at a merchant's named Bonacieux, as the name was known to me, I didn't hesitate and here I am.

D'ARTAGNAN

That's because they think the house is occupied by the Adjutant and his men and they want to make you fall into a trap, Milord. Milord, pardon me for having drawn a sword against you and tell me in what manner I can serve Your Grace.

BUCKINGHAM

Thanks, you're a brave chap. You offer me your services and I accept them. Walk behind us at twenty paces—accompany us to the Louvre—and—you know whose interests are concerned—if someone spies on us—kill them.

D'ARTAGNAN

That's excellent! Milord—go forward, I am with you.

BUCKINGHAM

Come, Madame.

D'ARTAGNAN

Planchet! Warn Porthos and Aramis that they cannot sleep to-night.

(Planchet exits through the window.)

CURTAIN

ACT II

Scene 6

Queen's chamber—the Louvre.

ANNE

Well, La Porte—the Duke?

LA PORTE

The Duke?

ANNE

You have no news of him?

LA PORTE

None can be had except from Madame Bonacieux and from the moment the Cardinal had her abducted, we fell into uncertainty.

ANNE

La Porte!

LA PORTE

Madame.

ANNE

It seems to me I hear someone walking in the secret corridor— see who it can be.

MADAME BONACIEUX

(opening the hidden door)

Silence!

ANNE

Ah, it's you, Constance!

MADAME BONACIEUX

Yes, Madame. Yes, Your Majesty, it's me.

ANNE

They set you at liberty?

MADAME BONACIEUX

I escaped.

ANNE

And you came here?

MADAME BONACIEUX

I have been where my presence was necessary.

ANNE

You have seen him?

MADAME BONACIEUX

Your Majesty.

ANNE

Reply quickly—you have seen him? No mischance has befallen him?

MADAME BONACIEUX

He is here.

ANNE

Here? Who?

MADAME BONACIEUX

The Duke.

ANNE

The Duke of Buckingham?

MADAME BONACIEUX

Himself.

ANNE

In the Louvre—near the King—near the Cardinal!

MADAME BONACIEUX

Madame, he said that since he had come, he was not going to return to London without seeing you—that he knew he had been drawn into a trap but that he thanked his enemies for putting him in this position.

ANNE

What madness! Return where you have left him—beg him—implore him, order him in my name.

(The Duke appears.)

Tell him that he must leave—that I will not see him—that I do not wish to see him—If necessary, I will tell everything to the King.

BUCKINGHAM

Oh—you haven't the courage, Madame.

ANNE

The Duke—La Porte, watch that side—Constance, the corridor—

(the Buckingham)

Oh sir—what have you done?

(The two servants distance themselves, the Queen and Buckingham remain alone.)

BUCKINGHAM

(going to one knee)

I came to kneel before you and say—Georges de Villiers, Duke of Buckingham is always the most humble and most obedient of your worshippers.

ANNE

Georges, you know it was not I who wrote you—right?

BUCKINGHAM

Yes, I know that I was made to believe that the snow would melt, that the marble grow warm—but what do you want? When one loves, one believes easily in love, besides I haven't lost by this voyage, since I see you.

ANNE

You forget, Milord, that in seeing me you run the risk of your life and you make me run a risk—a risk to my honor. You see me to hear me tell you that everything separates us:—the depths of the sea—the hostility of our two realms—the sanctity of oaths; it is a sacrilege to struggle against such things, Milord. You see me now to hear me tell you we can never see each other again.

BUCKINGHAM

Speak, Madame, speak Queen, the softness of your voice covers the hardness of your words. You speak of sacrilege. But the sacrilege is in the separation of hearts that God made for each other.

ANNE

Milord, I've never said that I love you.

BUCKINGHAM

But you've never said that you don't love me either.

ANNE

Milord!

BUCKINGHAM

And this will be a cruelty that you won't commit, for tell me— Queen—where will you find a love like mine? A love that neither time nor absence, nor despair, can extinguish—a love which contents itself with a ribbon, which cheers itself on a lost look, on an escaped word? It was three years ago that I saw you for the first time, Madame, and it's been three years since I loved you.

ANNE

Duke!

BUCKINGHAM

Do you want me to say how you were dressed the first time I saw you? Do you want me to list each ornament of your toilette? I still see you with this robe of satin embroidered with gold whose hanging sleeves are attached to your arms by strings of diamonds. Oh, yes, wait—I close my eyes and I see you as you were then—I open them and see you as you are—that's to say— a hundred times more beautiful.

ANNE

What madness to nourish such a hopeless passion with such memories!

BUCKINGHAM

And how do you expect me to live? I have only memories—they are my joy, my treasure, my hope. Each time that I see you it is one more diamond that I enclose in the casket of my heart. This is the fourth that you've allowed to fall and I picked up; for in three years, Madame, I've only seen you four times. The first as I've just told you, the second at the home of Madame de Chevreuse, the third in the gardens of Amiens.

ANNE

Don't speak of that night, Milord.

BUCKINGHAM

It's the most happy and radiant evening in my life. You recall what a beautiful night it was? How the air was soft and perfumed; how the heavens were blue and enameled with stars. Oh, that time, like today, I was alone with you—that time you were ready to tell me everything, your isolation in life, your heart's cares—the widowing of your soul—you were drawn to my arms—wait, this one—I felt, while inclining my head to your side, your beautiful hair stroking my face, and at each stroke, I trembled from head to foot. Oh, Queen, Queen, you don't know all the joy there is in such a moment. Take my wealth, my fortune, my glory—all that remains to me of days to live for such a night—for that night—oh—that night, Madame—you loved me!

ANNE

(rising)

But slander rose and spread from that night. The King, excited by the Cardinal, made a terrible uproar—Madame de Vernet was kicked out, Putange exiled, Madame de Chevreuse fell in disfavor—and when you wished to return as ambassador to France, the King himself opposed your return.

BUCKINGHAM

Yes, and France is going to pay with a war for that refusal by its King.

ANNE

Why's that?

BUCKINGHAM

I have no hope of entering Paris except in the hands of an army—no—without doubt—but this war can lead to a peace—the peace will need a negotiator—and I will be the negotiator—I will return to Paris, and I will see you again!

ANNE

Milord! But stop and think—all these proofs of love you wish to give me—they're crimes.

BUCKINGHAM

Ah, because you don't love me! Madame de Chevreuse of whom you spoke just now was less cold than you. Holland loves her and she has responded to his love.

ANNE

Alas, Madame de Chevreuse is not Queen.

BUCKINGHAM

Then you would love me if you weren't Queen, Madame? Oh, thanks for those soft words, O, my beautiful Majesty—a hundred thanks!

ANNE

Oh—you have twisted what I said.

BUCKINGHAM

I am happy in my error—so be it! Don't have the cruelty to take it from me. This letter from you; you said so yourself—they tried to trap me in a snare—I will let them have my life perhaps—for—wait—it's strange—for a long time—I've had a premonition I am going to die.

ANNE

Ah—my God!

BUCKINGHAM

I don't say this to frighten you—Madame—believe me, I don't preoccupy myself with such dreams—but this word you just said—this hope you have already given me—it must be paid for—perhaps with my life.

ANNE

Well, I too, Duke, I have premonitions, too, I had a dream—and in my dream I saw you in bed—bloody—wounded.

BUCKINGHAM

On the left side—with a knife—correct?

ANNE

Yes, that's it, Milord. Ah, my God—who told you that I had this dream? I have only spoken of it to God and only in my prayers.

(rising)

BUCKINGHAM

I can ask no more.

(on his knees)

You love me, Madame—all is well.

ANNE

I love you—me?

BUCKINGHAM

Yes, you! Would God send us the same dreams if you didn't love me? Would we have the same premonitions if our two beings weren't joined by the heart? You love me, Queen—and you cry for me.

ANNE

Oh, my God, you see this is more than I can bear. Wait, Duke, in the name of Heaven, leave—retire. I don't know if I love you or not—but what I do know is that if you were struck in France, that if you died in France, that if I thought your love for me was the cause of your death—I know I could never forgive myself—I know I would become mad! Leave, then leave, I beg you!

BUCKINGHAM

Oh, how beautiful you are this way—and how I love you—how I love you—

ANNE

Leave, leave and return later—return as ambassador, return as minister, surrounded by guards—who will defend you—with servants who will watch over you—and then, then—I won't fear for your life and I will be happy to see you.

BUCKINGHAM

Well—a proof of your indulgence—an object which will call me to you—and which will remind me that I haven't been dreaming, something you have worn and something that I can wear in my turn—a jewel—a collar—a necklace.

ANNE

And you will go? You will go, if I give you what you ask of me?

BUCKINGHAM

Yes.

ANNE

Right away?

BUCKINGHAM

Yes.

ANNE

You will leave France? You will return to England?

BUCKINGHAM

Yes, I swear it to you. I swear it to you.

ANNE

Wait, Milord, wait—

(She hurtles out of the room, Buckingham waits, immobile, arms folded. Anne reappears holding a box of rosewood.)

ANNE

Hold, Milord—hold—take this in memory of me—these are the diamonds that I wore the first time you saw me—and which the King gave me.

BUCKINGHAM

(falling on his knees)

Is it really true, Madame?

ANNE

You have promised me to leave.

BUCKINGHAM

And I am keeping my word—your hand, Madame, your hand. And I am leaving.

(Anne gives him her hand, which he kisses, transported.)

Before three months are over, Madame—I will be dead or I shall have seen you again, even if to do so I had to turn the world upside down.

MADAME BONACIEUX

(entering)

Madame! Madame!

ANNE

What's wrong?

MADAME BONACIEUX

The Duke was followed, his description taken, the password has been changed.

ANNE

You hear this, Duke?

BUCKINGHAM

My God—what is to be done!

D'ARTAGNAN

(entering quickly)

Put on this cap and hat, Milord, and yours there.

BUCKINGHAM

But the new password?

D'ARTAGNAN

Rochefort and La Rochelle, now don't forget that you are in the company of Mr. de Treville.

BUCKINGHAM

Madame.

ANNE

Leave, Duke, leave! In the name of heaven—leave.

MADAME BONACIEUX

Leave.

D'ARTAGNAN

Leave.

(The Duke leaves.)

ANNE

(listening)

Silence.

VOICE

Who goes there?

BUCKINGHAM

(outside)

From Mr. de Treville's company—Rochefort or La Rochelle.

VOICE

Pass.

ANNE

(falling in an armchair)

He is saved!

CURTAIN

ACT II

Scene 7

The Cardinal's office.

> *(A Court Clerk—the Cardinal behind a doorway.)*

COURT CLERK

My Lord can hear?

VOICE

> *(behind the tapestry)*

Yes.

COURT CLERK

Bring in the prisoner.

> *(Bonacieux is brought in by two guards.)*

COURT CLERK

Name, first name—age and domicile?

BONACIEUX

Jacques-Michel Bonacieux—age forty-one—spice merchant—Rue de Fossoyeurs.

COURT CLERK

You know, without doubt, why you are in the Bastille?

BONACIEUX

Because they brought me here, sir, without that, I swear I never myself—

COURT CLERK

You mistake my question or you pretend to mistake my question—I ask you if you are disposed to admit the crime for which you were brought to the Bastille.

BONACIEUX

A crime, sir! I—I have committed a crime?

COURT CLERK

You are accused most gravely of all—of the crime of high treason.

BONACIEUX

Of high treason? Eh, sir—how do you think a poor shopkeeper—who detests the Huguenots and abhors the Spanish—can be accused of high treason?

COURT CLERK

Mr. Bonacieux, you have a wife?

BONACIEUX

Ah! Yes, sir—that is to say I had one.

COURT CLERK

What—you had one? What have you done so you no longer have one?

BONACIEUX

They kidnapped her from me, sir.

COURT CLERK

And do you know who the man is who committed this rape?

BONACIEUX

Hum! I suspect a lord of high waist, black eyes—black hair and a scar on his temple.

COURT CLERK

(turning towards the screen)

Ah! Ah! And his name?

BONACIEUX

Oh—as to his name, I am ignorant of it—but if I ever meet him, I promise you I will recognize him even among a thousand people.

COURT CLERK

You would recognize him in a thousand, you say?

BONACIEUX

Pardon—I mean—

COURT CLERK

You answered you would recognize him—that's all.

BONACIEUX

Sir, I have not said I was sure. I said I believed so.

(During this, a man enters and whispers in the ear of the Clerk.)

COURT CLERK

Ah! Ah!

BONACIEUX

Let's see—is something still wrong?

COURT CLERK

It's that your affair is so complicated.

BONACIEUX

My affair?

COURT CLERK

What were you doing at Mr. D'Artagnan's, your neighbor—with whom you had a conference during the day?

BONACIEUX

Ah, yes, as to that, that's true, I was at Mr. D'Artagnan's.

COURT CLERK

What was the purpose of that visit?

BONACIEUX

To beg him to help me get my wife back—I believed I had the right to reclaim her—I deceived myself, sir.

COURT CLERK

And what reply did Mr. D'Artagnan make?

BONACIEUX

At first he promised me his help—but I soon saw that he was betraying me.

COURT CLERK

You lie, sir! Mr. D'Artagnan made a pact with you. He put to flight the police who had arrested your wife and he kept her from all attempts to retake her.

BONACIEUX

Mr. D'Artagnan has rescued my wife? Who told you that?

COURT CLERK

Happily, Mr. D'Artagnan is in our hands—and you are going to be confronted with him.

BONACIEUX

Ah, my word, I ask for nothing better. I won't be afraid to see a known face.

COURT CLERK

Bring in Mr. D'Artagnan.

BONACIEUX

Ah—now!

(Two guards lead in Athos.)

COURT CLERK

Mr. D'Artagnan, declare what took place between you and this gentleman.

BONACIEUX

But this is not Mr. D'Artagnan you are showing me.

COURT CLERK

What do you mean it isn't Mr. D'Artagnan?

BONACIEUX

Not the least in the world.

COURT CLERK

You dare to maintain?

BONACIEUX

Ah! Indeed, for goodness sake!

COURT CLERK

What do you call him if you don't call him D'Artagnan?

BONACIEUX

But I don't know his name—ask him—himself.

COURT CLERK

What is your name?

ATHOS

Athos.

COURT CLERK

That's not the name of a man—that's the name of a mountain.

ATHOS

It's my name.

COURT CLERK

Now you said you were named D'Artagnan.

ATHOS

Me?

COURT CLERK

Yes, you.

ATHOS

Oh, you mean when they said, "You are Mr. D'Artagnan!" and I said, "You think so?" My guards said they were sure—I didn't wish to contradict them, besides I might have deceived myself—I was drunk.

COURT CLERK

Sir, you insult the majesty of the law.

ATHOS

Not at all.

COURT CLERK

You are Mr. D'Artagnan.

ATHOS

You see, you said so again.

BONACIEUX

But I tell you, Mr. Commissioner, there is not a moment of doubt, Mr. D'Artagnan is my tenant—he hasn't paid me—and I ought to recognize him.

COURT CLERK

Well, that's a reason.

(to a messenger who gives him a letter)

What?

MESSENGER

Read!

COURT CLERK

(after having read it)

Oh, the poor wretched woman.

BONACIEUX

What are you saying? Of whom are you speaking—it isn't my wife, I hope?

COURT CLERK

On the contrary—it is about her—your affair is….

(sneering) All right—go.

BONACIEUX

(exasperated)

Ah, indeed, sir! Do me the pleasure of telling me in what way my affair can get worse than that of my wife while I am in prison.

COURT CLERK

Because what she does is the result of a plan concocted between you—an infernal plan.

BONACIEUX

I swear to you, Mr. Commissioner, that you are in the most profound error—I haven't the least idea in the world what my wife ought to do—and I am a complete stranger to what she has done—and if she has committed follies, I renounce her, I disown her, I curse her.

ATHOS

Ah then—if you have no further need of me, send me somewhere. He is very boring, your Mr. Bonacieux.

COURT CLERK

Take the prisoners back to their cells.

ATHOS

Now—if it's Mr. D'Artagnan you need to hold under lock and
key, I don't see why you put me in prison.

COURT CLERK

(to guards)

Do what I told you.

THE CARDINAL

One moment.

ALL

Monsignor.

ATHOS

(bowing)

Monsignor.

THE CARDINAL

You are free, Mr. Athos—

(to Bonacieux)

You stay—

(to guards)

leave us—

(Athos bows, all leave with marks of the most profound re-spect.)

BONACIEUX

Who is this gentleman who remains?

THE CARDINAL

You have conspired.

BONACIEUX

That's what they've already told me, Milord, but I swear to you that I know nothing.

THE CARDINAL

You have conspired with your wife, with Madame de Chevreuse, with Milord the Duke of Buckingham.

BONACIEUX

Ah—in fact, yes, Monsignor, yes—I have heard their names pronounced.

THE CARDINAL

By whom?

BONACIEUX

By Madame Bonacieux.

THE CARDINAL

On what occasion?

BONACIEUX

She said that the Cardinal Richelieu had lured the Duke of Buckingham to Paris, where he would be ruined and the Queen ruined with him.

THE CARDINAL

She said that?

BONACIEUX

Yes, Monsignor, but I told her that she was wrong to maintain such a proposition and that His Eminence was incapable—

THE CARDINAL

Shut up—you are an imbecile.

BONACIEUX

That's exactly what my wife replied, Monsignor.

THE CARDINAL

Do you know who has kidnapped your wife?

BONACIEUX

No, Monsignor.

THE CARDINAL

You have some suspicions, though?

BONACIEUX

Yes, Monsignor—but my suspicious appears to irritate the Commissioner and I no longer have them.

THE CARDINAL

When you went to search for your wife at the Louvre, did she return directly home?

BONACIEUX

For the last time, no—she had already some business with one of the silk merchants.

THE CARDINAL

And where do they live, these merchants of silk?

BONACIEUX

There's one in the Rue Vaugirard and the other in the Rue de la Harpe.

THE CARDINAL

Did you go inside these houses with her?

BONACIEUX

Never, Monsignor. I waited at the door.

THE CARDINAL

And what pretext did she give you for going in alone?

BONACIEUX

She didn't give any—she told me to wait and I waited.

THE CARDINAL

You're a compliant husband, my dear Mr. Bonacieux.

BONACIEUX

He calls me his dear Mister—that means things are going well.

THE CARDINAL

Would you recognize the doors of these houses?

BONACIEUX

Yes.

THE CARDINAL

Fine—someone—

(an officer enters)

Go fetch Rochefort—and the instant he's here, bring him in.

OFFICER

The Count is here, and asks to speak instantly to Your Eminence.

BONACIEUX

(aside, stupefied)

Eminence? Your Eminence, His Eminence.

CARDINAL

Let him come.

BONACIEUX

Oh, my God! You are the Cardinal, in person—Monsignor the Great Cardinal.

(he falls to his knees)

And I—

(He beats the floor with his head.)

CARDINAL

Come in, Rochefort.

ROCHEFORT

Monsignor.

BONACIEUX

It's him!

CARDINAL

Who—him?

BONACIEUX

The one who kidnapped my wife.

CARDINAL

(to Officer)

Put this man in the hands of the Guards.

BONACIEUX

No, Monsignor, no—it wasn't him—I was deceived—the gentleman doesn't resemble him at all. The gentleman is an honest man.

CARDINAL

Take this fool away!

(The take Bonacieux off who makes gestures of despair.)

ROCHEFORT

They were seen.

CARDINAL

The Queen and the Duke?

ROCHEFORT

Yes.

CARDINAL

Where?

ROCHEFORT

At the Louvre.

CARDINAL

Who told you this?

ROCHEFORT

Madame de Lannoy.

CARDINAL

Can she be counted on?

ROCHEFORT

She is entirely for Your Eminence.

CARDINAL

Very well—we are defeated—let's try to make our retreat.

ROCHEFORT

I will aid you with all my soul, Monsignor.

CARDINAL

What happened?

ROCHEFORT

At eleven o'clock the Queen was with her woman. She went into her boudoir and said, "Wait for me."

CARDINAL

And it was in the boudoir he was seen?

ROCHEFORT

Yes.

CARDINAL

Who brought him in?

ROCHEFORT

Madame Bonacieux.

CARDINAL

How much time did they remain together?

ROCHEFORT

A half hour—a little less.

CARDINAL

After that, the Queen returned?

ROCHEFORT

To take a box of rosewood and then she went out again soon.

CARDINAL

And when she came back—much later—did she bring back this box?

ROCHEFORT

No.

CARDINAL

Does Madame Lannoy know what was in the box?

ROCHEFORT

Strings of diamonds that the King gave to the Queen.

CARDINAL

Then she must have given them to the Duke?

ROCHEFORT

She gave them to him.

CARDINAL

You are quite sure, Rochefort?

ROCHEFORT

Perfectly sure.

CARDINAL

Fine, fine! All is not lost perhaps—and perhaps it is even for the best.

Now, do you know where Madame de Chevreuse and the Duke of Buckingham are?

ROCHEFORT

She's in the Rue de Vaugirard—he's at the Rue de la Harpe.

CARDINAL

That's excellent!

ROCHEFORT

Your Eminence wants me to arrest them?

CARDINAL

Oh—they're already gone.

ROCHEFORT

No matter—they can be caught.

CARDINAL

I have sent Vitrary with ten men—watch for his return and keep me up to date on all he's done.

ROCHEFORT

Be tranquil, Monsignor.

(He leaves.)

CARDINAL

Bring in the prisoner again.

(Bonacieux comes in.)

CARDINAL

You have deceived me.

BONACIEUX

Me—Monsignor—deceive Your Eminence?

CARDINAL

When your wife was going to the Rue de Vaugirard and the Rue de la Harpe, she wasn't going to silk merchants.

BONACIEUX

And where was she going then, by God?

CARDINAL

She was going to the Duchess de Chevreuse and to the Duke of Buckingham—the two mortal enemies of the King.

BONACIEUX

Yes, yes, that's it, Your Eminence is right—I told my wife many times that it was astonishing that silk merchants were living in houses without any sign—and each time my wife set herself to laughing—ah Monsignor, ah! That you are indeed the Cardinal, the Great Cardinal—the man of genius that Europe admires and who—

(throwing himself at the Cardinal's feet)

CARDINAL

(after having reflected)

Rise, my friend! You are a brave man.

(Bonacieux gets up.)

BONACIEUX

The Cardinal has touched my hand—I have touched the hand of a great man—the great man has called me his friend.

CARDINAL

Yes, my friend and as I suspected you unjustly, we must give you an indemnity. Here, take these hundred pistoles and pardon me.

BONACIEUX

How can I pardon you, Monsignor? But you were fully free to have me arrested—fully free to have me tortured—fully free to have me hanged. Pardon you, sir—come now, don't mention it.

CARDINAL

Goodbye then or rather till we meet again for we will see each other again, I hope.

BONACIEUX

Oh—as much as Monsignor wishes.

(He leaves.)

CARDINAL

Till we meet again, Mr. Bonacieux, till we meet again. There's a man who will, from this day forward, be ready to kill himself for me. Ah—it's you Rochefort—well?

ROCHEFORT

Well—no one. They're gone!

CARDINAL

Yes—one surely on to Tours, the other on the way to Boulogne—it's at London we will rejoin the Duke of Buckingham.

ROCHEFORT

Your orders, sir?

CARDINAL

Not a word of what has happened. Let the Queen remain in perfect security—let her believe that we were investigating the political conspiracy.

ROCHEFORT

Is that all?

CARDINAL

You will go to Milady—you will give her a rendezvous for the day after tomorrow at eleven o'clock in the evening at the Cabaret of Colombier Rouge where we've already seen each other twice—she will wait for me in her usual room and she will be prepared to take a trip. A chair will wait for her at the door.

ROCHEFORT

Yes, sir—and as for this man?

CARDINAL

What man?

ROCHEFORT

The imbecile they call Bonacieux—what's to be done with him, Your Eminence? I saw him leaving, radiant, and purse in hand counting gold.

CARDINAL

I have done all that can be done with him. I've made him a spy on his wife.

ROCHEFORT

And if Madame de Chevreuse returns to Paris?

THE KING

(entering)

What do you mean, if Madame de Chevreuse returns to Paris?—she's already been here.

CARDINAL

Your Majesty has heard—

(to Rochefort)

Leave us—but don't go far.

THE KING

Yes, Cardinal, I have heard. Ah! Madame de Chevreuse.

CARDINAL

For the last five days, sire, I am forced to admit it.

THE KING

Cardinal, there are some things that I cannot suffer.

CARDINAL

Sire, I attached little importance to this voyage until I learned—

THE KING

What have you learned, Cardinal?

CARDINAL

That Madame de Chevreuse had seen the Queen.

THE KING

They've seen each other?

ROCHEFORT

Yes, sir.

THE KING

Ah! Cardinal, there's a conspiracy.

CARDINAL

Yes, sire, and I would hold all the strings to this plot except that—

THE KING

Except what?

CARDINAL

But, as there's no more respect in France for the laws—as the sword settles all questions—as the service to Your Majesty is the pretext which covers up all violence, all criminal complicity.

THE KING

Cardinal, in what manner does my service shackle the laws? What's wrong?

CARDINAL

Just now, Sire, since you force me to speak—it happened that just as I was about to make an arrest sure of the fact, *in flagrante delicto*—possessed of all proofs—the emissary of Madame de Chevreuse and the Queen—when a musketeer, a guard—I don't know why—a soldier—intervened and dared to violently intercept the course of justice by falling, sword in hand, on the honest men of the police charged with examining the affair impartially and placing it before Your Majesty's eye.

THE KING

Truly—have they got accomplices among my servants?

CARDINAL

Sire—be calm.

THE KING

I will be calm when I know everything—ah—they have recourse to my Musketeers! Ah—they use my guards against me—against my honor—we will see about that!

(He makes towards the Queen's apartment.)

CARDINAL

Pardon—but where is Your Majesty going?

THE KING

Where am I going—'S'death—I'm going to see the Queen.

CARDINAL

I still have some words to put to Your Majesty.

THE KING

Speak quickly.

CARDINAL

At the same time Madame de Chevreuse was here—the Duke was in Paris.

THE KING

What duke?

CARDINAL

The Duke of Buckingham.

THE KING

The Duke of Buckingham—what did he come here for?

CARDINAL

He came, without doubt to conspire with the Spanish and the Huguenots—to prepare this formidable expedition against La Rochelle.

THE KING

No—to conspire against my honor.

CARDINAL

Your Majesty tells me this after the reports of Madame Lannoy.

THE KING

What reports?

CARDINAL

Madame Lannoy must have told Your Majesty that the Queen woke very late and this morning cried much while writing by herself.

THE KING

She cried—she wrote—but these letters—these letters that she wrote have already been sent perhaps?

CARDINAL

It doesn't seem so, Sire—Madame Lannoy would have told me.

THE KING

These letters—they must be had.

CARDINAL

Oh! Sire!

THE KING

And as for this Englishman—as for this infamous Duke of Buckingham, why haven't you had him arrested?

CARDINAL

To arrest the Duke—to arrest the Prime Minister of King Charles—what are you thinking of, sir?

THE KING

Well—instead of arresting him—let him be exposed like a spy—
we must—

CARDINAL

We must—?

THE KING

Nothing—nothing—but what's he doing?

CARDINAL

He's gone, Sire—he left Paris last night.

THE KING

Are you sure they didn't meet?

CARDINAL

Oh—I believe the Queen is very much attached to Your Majesty.

THE KING

While awaiting, they corresponded—she wrote—wrote while
crying—Cardinal—I repeat to you I must have those letters—I
want them!

CARDINAL

Such a mission, Sire, will embarrass all Your Majesty's subjects,
for if the King says "I want them" the Queen can say—"I don't
want to give them up!"

THE KING

We are going to see if she will disobey me.

(He rings—an usher presents himself.)

THE KING

Tell the Queen that I beg her to come here.

(The usher leaves.)

CARDINAL

I will retire.

THE KING

Don't you go far. Ah, Chancellor is working my large office—send him to me.

(The Cardinal leaves, bowing to the Queen.)

(The Queen enters.)

ANNE

(aside)

The Cardinal, my God!

(aloud)

Your Majesty has done me the honor of asking for me?

THE KING

Yes, Madame.

ANNE

I await Your Majesty's orders.

THE KING

Less respect, Madame, and more frankness—why is Madame de Chevreuse in Paris?

ANNE

Heavens! Madame de Chevreuse! I don't know, Sire.

THE KING

Why—last night—were you up so late?

ANNE

(aside)

I feel I'm dying.

THE KING

Why were you crying? Why were you writing?

ANNE

I assure you—

THE KING

You were writing! To whom—Madame?

ANNE

Sire.

THE KING

That letter—you haven't sent it to its addressee—where is it? I want it!

ANNE

Your Majesty didn't marry a princess of my name to make her a slave.

THE KING

Yes, go ahead—rebel! I prefer that to your hypocritical respect—
that letter—

ANNE

What I write—is mine.

THE KING

What you write—is your King's—your master's—do you intend
to give this letter?

ANNE

Reflect, Sire.

(Enters the Chancellor.)

THE KING

Ah—enter Chancellor.

(to the Queen)

Madame—you refuse.

ANNE

Yes.

THE KING

For the last time, that letter!

ANNE

Never.

THE KING

Chancellor, you are the first magistrate of my realm—you know the crimes of treason and *lèse-majesté*—you will enter into Madame's apartment—the Queen's apartment and make an exact investigation of all her papers which you will bring here to me.

ANNE

Infamy!

THE KING

Your keys, Madame.

ANNE

The Chancellor shall command—and Doña Estefana—my chamber maid will give the keys to my tables and secretaries.

THE KING

Go, sir.

(The Chancellor leaves.)

THE KING

Oh—you are very calm, Madame, very proud, you know the Chancellor will find nothing—in fact, it's not to a drawer of furniture that one confides the type of letter you have written.

ANNE

What do you mean to say, sir?

THE KING

When I punished this traitor—this rebel they called the Marshall d'Ancre killed him—they found the proofs of his crimes at the home of his wife—she hadn't confided them to her drawers or tables—but in searching her—

ANNE

The Marshall d'Ancre—a Florentine adventurer, that's all—but the spouse of Your Majesty is called Anne of Austria. She is the daughter of a King—the most important princess in the world.

THE KING

And as such, Anne of Austria is only more guilty—one cannot treat guilty people nicely.

(he takes a step)

That letter!

ANNE

I will call my brother!

THE KING

I have armies to reply to him—this letter.

ANNE

I will call on the honor of French gentlemen.

THE KING

Think first of mine! This letter, I tell you—you are hiding it—you are hiding it on your person. Give it to me!

ANNE

Sire!

THE KING

Give it to me! Or I will take it.

ANNE

I will spare you that shame, Sire, I will spare myself this af-
front—well, yes, I wrote a letter.

THE KING

Ah—you admit it?

ANNE

This letter—your Chancellor will not find it. I have it on me—as
you said. You wish it?

THE KING

I wish it.

ANNE

Here it is!

(She falls into an armchair.)

THE KING

(opening the letter cautiously)

"My Brother."

(speaking)

She's writing to the King of Spain.

(reading)

"Complaints against the Cardinal—a league of Spain and Austria
with the end of overthrowing my minister."

(Enter the Cardinal.)

CARDINAL

Some politics—right, sire?

THE KING

Yes, Cardinal—nothing but politics; not a word about what I thought—God be praised—hold.

CARDINAL

(reading)

"I was quite sure I told Your Majesty so—"

THE KING

Never mind! It was a conspiracy against you and the Queen didn't deserve my wrath any less.

CARDINAL

Oh! Sire! The Queen is my enemy—but isn't she a submissive, irreproachable spouse? Let me intercede for her.

ANNE

What's he say?

THE KING

Well—let her return to me first.

CARDINAL

On the contrary, Sire, give her an example—you were wrong first—since you suspected the Queen—and because you provoked a scandal.

THE KING

Well—what's to be done?

CARDINAL

Something which must be agreeable to Her Majesty, the Queen, something which must be a distraction and a reparation at the same time. Give a ball—or rather the Aldermen of the city of Paris are giving a ball in a few days—it would be a great honor for them to receive Your Majesties.

THE KING

When is it?

CARDINAL

In four days—I believe, Sire. It will be, I tell you, a great joy for the city and it will be an occasion for Her Majesty, the Queen, to wear those beautiful diamonds that the King gave her.

ANNE

Oh, my God!

THE KING

You're right, Cardinal—you're right—this—Madame—you accept, right?

CARDINAL

(low to King)

Your Majesty will insist that the Queen appears in the diamonds.

(Cardinal exits.)

THE KING

What's he mean? Is he preparing one of those terrible surprises for me that he knows how to make?

(to the Queen)

You haven't said that you accept, Madame—are you listening?

ANNE

Yes, Sire, I'm listening.

THE KING

You will appear at this ball which takes place in four days?

ANNE

Yes.

THE KING

With diamonds?

ANNE

Yes.

THE KING

Fine, I'm counting on it. Counting on it. Goodbye, Madame.

(He leaves.)

ANNE

(aside)

I'm lost.

(Enter Madame Bonacieux.)

MADAME BONACIEUX

Can I do nothing for my Queen?

ANNE

You! You!

MADAME BONACIEUX

Oh, I am with you body and soul—and however far I am from Your Majesty, I will find a way to save her.

ANNE

Me—betrayed on all sides, sold, ruined?

MADAME BONACIEUX

These diamonds which the King demands.

ANNE

You know?

MADAME BONACIEUX

I heard everything. These diamonds were in the little rosewood box?

ANNE

Yes!

MADAME BONACIEUX

That box—Milord Buckingham—didn't he take it away with him yesterday?

ANNE

Silence! Silence!

MADAME BONACIEUX

It's necessary to get them back.

ANNE

But how?

MADAME BONACIEUX

We must send someone to the Duke.

ANNE

Why, my God! Who?

MADAME BONACIEUX

Have you faith in me, Madame? If you do me this honor, my Queen—I have found the messenger!

ANNE

Do it!—and you save my life and my honor.

MADAME BONACIEUX

But the Duke will not give up those diamonds without a word from your hand.

ANNE

A word from my hand? If that is discovered—for me it's divorce—the convent, exile.

MADAME BONACIEUX

And for me it's death.

(Anne runs to the table and writes while Madame Bonacieux watches the doors.)

ANNE

Here!

MADAME BONACIEUX

Good, Madame.

ANNE

But your messenger—they will arrest him—they will attack him—he will never arrive on time.

MADAME BONACIEUX

The one I am sending, Madame, if they arrest him, he'll pass through, if they attack him, he'll kill them—Oh—you will see—goodbye, Madame—goodbye.

CURTAIN

ACT III

Scene 8

D'Artagnan's Room.

> *(Planchet, flat on his face, drawing a bottle from the trap-door. Athos enters and takes the bottle which Planchet places by him.)*

ATHOS

Thanks, Planchet, a glass.

PLANCHET

Ah, Mr. Athos—truly, is it you? My God, how happy I am to see you. A glass—two if you like. Then you've been released from the Bastille?

ATHOS

You see it's quite so, since I am here.

PLANCHET

I thought I had locked the door with a key.

ATHOS

You know that we each have a key to our respective apartments.

PLANCHET

Ah—that's true.

ATHOS

And your master—where is he?

PLANCHET

Ah, sir—I am not uneasy.

ATHOS

Ah—you're not uneasy.

PLANCHET

No—the Chevalier is in good fortune—everything's been patched up.

ATHOS

Patched up? With who?

PLANCHET

With this naughty woman, you know?

ATHOS

Which one?

PLANCHET

The one called Milady; the woman of the Palace Royale.

ATHOS

Did he say something to you in parting?

PLANCHET

He said that if he didn't return tomorrow morning by nine o'clock, I should advise you, Mr. Porthos, and Mr. Aramis, and that you should take counsel.

ATHOS

Ah, the devil!

PLANCHET

Hush! Listen!

ATHOS

What?

PLANCHET

It seems to me I hear a noise on the stairs.

ATHOS

Sir.

D'ARTAGNAN

(outside and pushing the door)

Planchet—'S'death, Planchet—will you open, you clown?

PLANCHET

Something's going on—it's him—it's the Chevalier.

ATHOS

Oh! Oh! What's the matter with him?

D'ARTAGNAN

Ah, a thousand demons.

PLANCHET

Are you being pursued?

D'ARTAGNAN

(entering all upset)

I don't know, but lock the door.

ATHOS

Well, D'Artagnan?

D'ARTAGNAN

Athos—you, my friend? You are then free from their clutches?

ATHOS

Yes, and I came to pay you my first visit.

D'ARTAGNAN

It's God who inspired you. I was going to run to you.

ATHOS

What's happened?

D'ARTAGNAN

What has happened? Planchet, guard the stairway and don't let a living soul enter.

PLANCHET

Except the ladies.

D'ARTAGNAN

Ladies, less than anyone, 'S'death.

ATHOS

Ah! It appears that our loves have turned out badly?

D'ARTAGNAN

Athos; don't laugh—on, no for by Heaven don't laugh—for—on my soul—there's nothing to laugh about.

ATHOS

In fact, you're very pale—were you injured?

D'ARTAGNAN

No, thank God!

ATHOS

What's wrong then?

D'ARTAGNAN

I was afraid—

ATHOS

You, D'Artagnan—D'Artagnan afraid? What happened then?

D'ARTAGNAN

A terrible thing, Athos!

ATHOS

Explain yourself—what is it?

D'ARTAGNAN

It's that Milady is branded with a fleur de lys on her shoulder.

ATHOS

Ah! Milady branded—who told you that?

D'ARTAGNAN

Look here, answer me! Are you sure the other one is dead?

ATHOS

The other one?

D'ARTAGNAN

The one you told me about the other day—here—in this place—the woman from Berry.

ATHOS

(passing his hand before his face)

Who is Milady? Her age—her figure—her appearance?

D'ARTAGNAN

Twenty-five to twenty-six years of age, small rather than large—silky brown hair—eyebrows very marked—eyes somber and full of sparks.

ATHOS

Pale?

D'ARTAGNAN

Pale—magnificent shoulders and on the left a red fleur de lys, somewhat effaced under layers of makeup.

ATHOS

You said she's English.

D'ARTAGNAN

Well—yours—what was she?

ATHOS

That's true—Charlotte Backson. How did you know her?

D'ARTAGNAN

The woman saw she pleased me. She's a coquette, she made me advances. I accepted them—suddenly—the chambermaid took a pretty passion for my person and warned me that her mistress was mocking me. I am from the Midi—rage went to my head—I demanded proofs and she proved to me that Milady was giving a rendezvous to a Mr. de Vardes at her home. "I will avenge myself in a terrible way," I shouted. The chambermaid would refuse me nothing and I ordered her to place me in her mistress' apartment. It was easy—Milady was waiting for her lover and the chamber was without light.

ATHOS

Without light?

D'ARTAGNAN

Naturally—because of the fleur de lys, by God! Well—I entered and my business was proceeding marvelously, when suddenly the maid, jealous and fearing that my vengeance was much softer than I had announced, pretended to have been called and appeared with a light in her hand—Milady recognized me—she wanted to make me leave—I refused, and in the struggle, her peignoir was torn.

ATHOS

Ah—and you saw her shoulder?

D'ARTAGNAN

My friend—shut me in with an enraged panther—with a furious lioness—with a rattlesnake—I will consent to it—but with this woman who followed me, dagger in hand—Athos, I've told you all in two words, here even beside you, just thinking of her I'm afraid.

ATHOS

Wait—what have you there on your finger?

D'ARTAGNAN

A ring that she put there thinking I was Vardes.

ATHOS

This ring?

D'ARTAGNAN

I haven't even looked at it.

ATHOS

I know it—it's the one I gave her the evening of our wedding—D'Artagnan—it is she!

D'ARTAGNAN

In that case, my dear Athos, I'm afraid of having drawn a terrible vengeance on both of us.

ATHOS

What matter to me?

D'ARTAGNAN

What do you mean—what's it matter to you?

ATHOS

On my soul, D'Artagnan, I would give my life for a hair. But you alarm yourself needlessly on my account. She believes me dead as I believed her to be.

D'ARTAGNAN

Athos, there's a horrible mystery of some sort in all this. She's ready to take a trip—wait, I don't know why, but I am convinced this woman is a spy for the Cardinal.

ATHOS

(taking his cloak)

That's perfect.

D'ARTAGNAN

You are leaving me.

ATHOS

She lives in the Palace Royale, doesn't she?

D'ARTAGNAN

Yes, on the corner at the left bank.

ATHOS

Marvelous.

D'ARTAGNAN

A last word—while you're going, send Porthos to me—and Aramis—we may perhaps need all our forces in the face of the enemy.

ATHOS

Fine.

D'ARTAGNAN

Go.

(Exit Athos.)

D'ARTAGNAN

Ouf—here are adventures! Without counting that I don't know the end of it.

A VOICE

Mr. D'Artagnan, Mr. D'Artagnan.

D'ARTAGNAN

Didn't I just hear my name?

(Knocking under D'Artagnan's feet.)

VOICE

Mr. D'Artagnan.

D'ARTAGNAN

(opening the trap door)

Who's calling me?

MADAME BONACIEUX

Me, Madame Bonacieux. Are you alone?

D'ARTAGNAN

Yes, do you want me to come down?

MADAME BONACIEUX

No—I'll come up to you—can you receive me?

D'ARTAGNAN

By God!

MADAME BONACIEUX

Close the trap-door then.

(He closes the trap door.)

D'ARTAGNAN

If I can receive her! I think so, the adorable creature—let her come—'S'death.

(going to the door)

Let her pass, Planchet.

(Enter Madame Bonacieux.)

MADAME BONACIEUX

Ah, my God—I am dying.

PLANCHET

Sir, must I still do guard duty?

D'ARTAGNAN

More so than ever, Planchet.

MADAME BONACIEUX

Mr. D'Artagnan—ah—what a joy to meet you again.

D'ARTAGNAN

Here I am, Madame.

MADAME BONACIEUX

You have offered me your services.

D'ARTAGNAN

And I offer them to you again.

MADAME BONACIEUX

So much the better for I have answered for you.

D'ARTAGNAN

To whom?

MADAME BONACIEUX

To the Queen.

D'ARTAGNAN

You have done well—I am at her orders and yours.

MADAME BONACIEUX

Sir, I hardly know you—but I have complete confidence in you—why? I don't know.

D'ARTAGNAN

I know why. It's because I love you.

MADAME BONACIEUX

You tell me so. Listen to me. I swear before God, that if you betray me and my enemies spare me, which I doubt, I swear, I swear that I will kill myself and accuse you of my death.

D'ARTAGNAN

And as for me, before God, I too swear, Madame, that if I am taken in carrying out the orders you give me—that I will die before doing or saying anything that might compromise someone I respect or love.

MADAME BONACIEUX

Well—it's a question of leaving this instant without losing a second.

D'ARTAGNAN

For what country?

MADAME BONACIEUX

For London—and to take this letter.

D'ARTAGNAN

To whom?

MADAME BONACIEUX

To the Duke of Buckingham.

D'ARTAGNAN

But I must have leave from Mr. de Treville.

MADAME BONACIEUX

I stopped by him—in a quarter of an hour, your leave will be here.

D'ARTAGNAN

I will leave—but—on my return!

MADAME BONACIEUX

On your return?

D'ARTAGNAN

What will Madame Bonacieux do for the man who risks his life for her?

MADAME BONACIEUX

Silence!

D'ARTAGNAN

What?

MADAME BONACIEUX

The voice of my husband.

D'ARTAGNAN

Be easy. Planchet is guarding the door. What will you do? Speak.

MADAME BONACIEUX

I don't know—but come to meet her wherever she may be and we will see.

D'ARTAGNAN

But where will she be?

MADAME BONACIEUX

You will ask her of the Queen—and the Queen will tell you; this will be your reward.

BONACIEUX

(on the other side of the door)

But when I tell you that it is not to Mr. D'Artagnan that I wish to speak, but to my wife—

MADAME BONACIEUX

Save yourself—I will stay here.

D'ARTAGNAN

(opening the Judas)

Through here?

MADAME BONACIEUX

Have you money?

D'ARTAGNAN

I have enough.

(They embrace.)

MADAME BONACIEUX

Well, what are you doing now?

D'ARTAGNAN

I am taking some earnest money for my trip.

MADAME BONACIEUX

But you haven't left yet.

(D'Artagnan descends by the Judas.)

PLANCHET

(outside)

What do you mean, to your wife?

BONACIEUX

(outside, too)

Yes, I know my wife is with Mr. D'Artagnan and I wish to speak to her—what the Devil! I have the right to speak to my wife—

Ah, Mr. Planchet—Mr. Planchet—I warn you if you don't open, I am going to fetch the police.

MADAME BONACIEUX

(opening the door)

But let him enter, Mr. Planchet, since my husband wishes to speak to me, let him speak.

BONACIEUX

This is very fortunate! What are you doing here, Madame?

MADAME BONACIEUX

I am awaiting Mr. D'Artagnan.

BONACIEUX

Mr. D'Artagnan, you are waiting for Mr. D'Artagnan. Hum! Hum!

MADAME BONACIEUX

Without doubt, you can see he isn't here.

BONACIEUX

Ah—he isn't here.

MADAME BONACIEUX

Damnation, it seems so to me.

BONACIEUX

It's true. But why are you waiting for Mr. D'Artagnan?

MADAME BONACIEUX

Ah—Mr. Bonacieux, it's a matter that doesn't concern you.

BONACIEUX

What do you mean this doesn't concern me? And who does it concern, I ask you?

MADAME BONACIEUX

It concerns people you don't know and with whom you have no business.

BONACIEUX

(crossing his arms)

Yes—doesn't this concern Madame de Chevreuse and the Duke of Buckingham?

MADAME BONACIEUX

What are you talking about, my God!

BONACIEUX

Ah, Madame, you didn't know I knew about your conspiracy.

MADAME BONACIEUX

What names you're using—and who told you—?

BONACIEUX

Intrigues—isn't it always intrigues? But I am on my guard now against your intrigues, and the Cardinal has enlightened me about them.

MADAME BONACIEUX

The Cardinal—you have seen the Cardinal?

BONACIEUX

(importantly)

He called me, Madame.

MADAME BONACIEUX

And you responded to his invitation—imprudent fool that you are.

BONACIEUX

I must say I had no choice about responding or not responding, attended as I was by two guards.

MADAME BONACIEUX

Then he mistreated you—he threatened you.

BONACIEUX

He gave me his hand and called me his friend—do you grasp, Madame, that I am the friend of the great Cardinal?

MADAME BONACIEUX

Of the Great Cardinal! There are powers greater than he.

BONACIEUX

I am angry, Madame, but I don't know of any power greater than those of that great man I have the honor to serve.

MADAME BONACIEUX

You serve the Cardinal? It only lacked for you to serve the party of those who mistreat your wife and who insult your Queen.

(During the last lines of this scene Porthos and Aramis with their lackeys are quietly admitted by Planchet.)

BONACIEUX

Madame, the Queen is a perfidious Spaniard, and what the Cardinal does is well done.

MADAME BONACIEUX

Ah, sir, I knew you were cowardly, avaricious, imbecile, but I
never knew you were infamous.

BONACIEUX

Huh? What are you saying there?

MADAME BONACIEUX

I say the only thing lacking is for you to follow me and spy on
me.

BONACIEUX

That's exactly what I have done. That's exactly what I am going
to do.

MADAME BONACIEUX

What—you're going to report to the Cardinal?

BONACIEUX

That I found you at Mr. D'Artagnan's and that you wouldn't tell
me your reason for being here and that I can only think you are
conspiring with him.

MADAME BONACIEUX

You are gong to do that? Oh, no—impossible.

BONACIEUX

With this foot, Madame, with this foot, I am going there.

MADAME BONACIEUX

Oh—there's a justice and God will not permit it—

BONACIEUX

Ah!—God, the Cardinal is in touch with him and he will make it his business.

PORTHOS and ARAMIS

Excuse us, brave man, but no one can leave.

BONACIEUX

What—one cannot pass?

ARAMIS

It's orders, you know, sir—the Musketeers are slaves of their orders.

BONACIEUX

And who has given you this order?

PORTHOS

Our friend, D'Artagnan.

BONACIEUX

And he isn't here, your friend, D'Artagnan?

D'ARTAGNAN

(pushing his body up the trap)

Pardon, my dear, Bonacieux, you are wrong—here I am.

BONACIEUX

Mr. D'Artagnan—half in his place, half in mine.

PORTHOS

What's to be done, Brigadier?

D'ARTAGNAN

Take the greatest care of Mr. Bonacieux—don't let him want anything—but lock him in the cellar—and don't let him leave until my return—Planchet, Bazin and Mousqueton will watch him—that's the order.

BONACIEUX

As for your return—and when are you coming back?

D'ARTAGNAN

I don't know—adieu.

MADAME BONACIEUX

This will teach you, sir, to play spy for the Cardinal.

CURTAIN

ACT III

Scene 9

The Inn of the Colombier Rouge. Street floor and second floor.

(Milady is writing—Athos is with the host on the street-floor.)

ATHOS

But it seems to me there is nothing very extraordinary in what I told you there—I am waiting for two of my friends—we wish to get drunk together—we are afraid we will be disturbed in this respectable operation and we wish to rent this room.

HOST

No, that isn't what I understood—I thought you wanted to rent the whole house—understand that as the second floor is already occupied—

ATHOS

Well yes, by a woman—you have told me. We are very gallant to disturb ladies—what the devil—let this lady stay where she is—and since only we can dispose of this room—

HOST

Very good—in this way, everything will arrange itself, my God! And in return for pistoles—

ATHOS

Here—bring us wine.

HOST

How many bottles?

ATHOS

As many as you like.

HOST

(aside)

Famous way of doing things!

(He leaves.)

ATHOS

She's here—I saw her go in—I hear her walk above me.

MILADY

(going to the window)

The Cardinal said "at 10:30".

(Ten o'clock sounds)

Come on, it's not he who is late—it's I who am ahead of my time.

PORTHOS

(arriving outside to Athos)

Hush!

ATHOS

Well?

PORTHOS

Aramis gave the signal.

ATHOS

Then they are coming?

PORTHOS

Yes.

ATHOS

So be it.

PORTHOS

Now—can't you tell me?

ATHOS

Useless—I want to know only one thing.

PORTHOS

Which is?

ATHOS

It's how I can hear what is said upstairs.

HOST

(entering)

Here's the wine.

ATHOS

Thanks. We are comfy and nobody will disturb us?

HOST

No—ah, only one piece of advice.

ATHOS

Which is?

HOST

Not to make a fire in the stove.

ATHOS

Why's that?

HOST

You are going to understand. I am a smart fellow—I've killed two birds with one stone—with the stove I'm heating the ground floor, with the chimney, the place above—but yesterday the chimney collapsed, yes, in a row, in a dispute, in a fire—so that if you light a fire you'll smoke her out.

ATHOS

Who?

HOST

The little lady on the second floor—who took the chamber above for herself alone.

ATHOS

For her—all by herself?

HOST

Yes and for a cavalier who must soon join her.

ATHOS

Hush—that's not our concern.

HOST

Bravo! Here's your wine. If you don't have enough, ask for more!

(He leaves—at the door he meets Rochefort.)

(Rochefort enters at the back door.)

ROCHEFORT

Here, friend!

HOST

What's wrong?

ROCHEFORT

This inn—is this the Colombier Rouge?

HOST

You can see for yourself.

ROCHEFORT

You have on the second floor a lady who is waiting?

HOST

Are you the person?

ROCHEFORT

No.

HOST

Well, then?

ROCHEFORT

Silence!

(goes to the back and addresses the Cardinal who waits outside enveloped in a cloak and escorted by two guards)

Come Monsignor.

CARDINAL

She's come?

ROCHEFORT

She's waiting for Your Eminence.

CARDINAL

Show me the way.

HOST

Oh, you cannot miss it. Take this staircase—follow the outside balcony—first door to the left.

CARDINAL

Thanks.

(He goes up.)

ROCHEFORT

(to the host)

Now, my friend, go about your business.

HOST

About my business?

ROCHEFORT

Yes, you must have some, go.

MILADY

(at the window)

Come, Monsignor, this way!

(Athos listens at the door. Aramis knocks at the side window.)

ATHOS

See who's knocking at the window, Porthos.

ARAMIS

(outside)

It's me, Aramis.

ATHOS

Porthos—open it.

(Aramis enters through the window.)

PORTHOS

Why did you come in through the window?

ARAMIS

Because it would be dangerous to come in through the door.

ATHOS

(to Aramis)

Have you seen the leader of the gang?

ARAMIS

Yes, by the rays of the moon he opened his cloak a single instant but that sufficed.

ATHOS

It's the Cardinal, right?

ARAMIS

It's the Cardinal.

PORTHOS

The Cardinal? Oh!

ATHOS

And the others?

ARAMIS

The Count de Rochefort and two guards of His Eminence—and as they are there, I came in through the window—so as not to be seen by them.

PORTHOS

I understand! And when I think I had no idea.

ATHOS

He's above—Porthos—lift the stove and put it somewhere.

PORTHOS

The stove?

ATHOS

Do it, I beg you.

(Porthos moves the stove.)

MILADY

Oh—now we are quite alone, Monsignor—fear nothing.

CARDINAL

No matter—we cannot take too many precautions.

ATHOS

(listening by the chimney)

A veritable listening tube.

ARAMIS

You can hear what they are saying.

ATHOS

I won't lose a word of it.

PORTHOS

Ah, I understand—that's why you told me—

ATHOS

Porthos, drink this wine or empty the bottles out the window.

PORTHOS

Empty the bottles?

ATHOS

We must appear to have consumed the wine.

PORTHOS

Yes, yes, yes.

CARDINAL

Let's sit down, Milady, and discuss these matters.

ATHOS

Hush.

MILADY

I'm listening, Your Eminence.

ATHOS

Oh—that voice.

CARDINAL

You know the importance of the mission that has been confided to you?

MILADY

Yes, but deign to give me my instructions clearly, Monsignor—I want to justify your confidence.

ATHOS

Lock the door, Aramis.

CARDINAL

You are going to leave for London.

MILADY

If you are sending me to the Duke of Buckingham, Monsignor, be careful. I am the one who presented him with the handkerchief in the Rue de la Harpe, that letter Madame Bonacieux was to present—he can easily recognize me.

CARDINAL

Little importance—it wouldn't even be bad if he knew you were in my employ.

MILADY

Then it's an open negotiation that I undertake, and I can present myself openly and honestly to him.

CARDINAL

Yes, open and honestly—as always.

MILADY

Speak, Monsignor—I will follow to the letter the order of Your Eminence.

ARAMIS

(to Porthos who has uncorked a bottle)

Hush, Porthos.

PORTHOS

But Athos told me to empty the bottles and I am emptying them.

CARDINAL

You are going to find Buckingham for me—you will tell him
that I know all the preparations he's made, but that I am not uneasy—waiting for his first movement, I will destroy the Queen.

MILADY

Will he believe Your Eminence can carry out this threat?

CARDINAL

You will tell him that I have some proofs, and when he learns
that this war he's undertaking can cost the honor and the liberty
of the lady of his thoughts, I tell you he'll think twice about it.

MILADY

And yet—if he persists?

CARDINAL

It's not probable.

MILADY

It's possible.

CARDINAL

If he persists? Well, I shall put my faith in one of those events
that change the face of States.

MILADY

Your Eminence means to say Ravaillac's knife thrust?

CARDINAL

Exactly.

MILADY

But, Your Eminence doesn't fear that the fate of Ravaillac won't frighten those who for a moment have the intention of imitating him?

CARDINAL

There are, in all times and in all countries, especially in countries divided in religion—like England for example—there are, I say, some fanatics who ask nothing better than the opportunity to make martyrs of themselves.

MILADY

Ah—you believe one can find such men?

CARDINAL

Right—exactly—the ship you are going to take at Boulogne to go to London is a merchant sloop commanded by a man of this type.

MILADY

You know him to be an enemy of Milord?

CARDINAL

Oh—of long standing.

MILADY

What's his name?

CARDINAL

Felton.

MILADY

Ah—

CARDINAL

This Felton, under his mask of Puritanism, hides a soul on fire; it would only take a woman—young, beautiful—adroit—to turn the head of such a man.

MILADY

Yes—and this woman can be found?

CARDINAL

Well—such a woman—who would put the dagger of a Jacques Clement or of a Ravaillac in the hands of this fanatic—this woman would save France.

MILADY

Yes, but she would be the accomplice of an assassin.

CARDINAL

What would it take to reassure her?

MILADY

I believe that it would be necessary for her to have a decree that ratified in advance whatever measures she believed necessary to take for the good of France.

CARDINAL

The thing is to find this woman.

MILADY

I will find her.

CARDINAL

These things will go marvelously if this man is found by me and this woman by you.

MILADY

Yes—there only remains a decree.

CARDINAL

A decree like this.

(he writes a decree)

MILADY

Yes, and now that I have received Monsignor's instructions concerning his enemies, I mean the enemies of France—His Eminence will permit me to tell him two words of mine?

CARDINAL

You have some enemies then?

MILADY

Yes, Monsignor—and some enemies against whom you ought to lend me your aid, for I made them in serving Your Eminence.

CARDINAL

Name them to me.

MILADY

There's this little intriguing Madame Bonacieux.

CARDINAL

Ah—ah—the Queen suspects something on that subject—for she sent her tonight to the convent of Béthune—the Carmelites.

MILADY

The Carmelites of Béthune.

CARDINAL

You know the country?

MILADY

I'd lived there—the other enemy.

CARDINAL

Ah—there are two—?

MILADY

The other—Your Eminence—knows him well—he's our bad genius—the one who in the meeting with Your Eminence's guards so cruelly wounded Mr. de Jussac. He's the one who, when all was prepared to capture the Duke in the house in the Rue des Fossoyeurs, came and put to flight Your Eminence's agents and caused us to fail.

CARDINAL

Ah—I know of whom you mean to speak.

MILADY

I wish to speak of this wretched D'Artagnan.

CARDINAL

He's a bold companion!

MILADY

Only the more to be feared—

CARDINAL

But I need proof of his communications with Buckingham.

MILADY

Some proof? I will have ten.

CARDINAL

Oh—but then the thing is very simple—give me some proof and I will send him to the Bastille.

MILADY

What follows?

CARDINAL

When one is in the Bastille, nothing follows.

MILADY

Monsignor, swap for swap, existence for existence, man for man, give me D'Artagnan, and I will give you Buckingham.

CARDINAL

I don't know what you mean, Milady—but as I have the desire to be agreeable to you, here's the paper you've asked of me.

MILADY

Thanks, Monsignor.

PORTHOS

Have you heard?

ARAMIS

Oh, the atrocious creature.

ATHOS

Fine—don't budge.

PORTHOS

What?

ATHOS

The rest concerns me.

ARAMIS

You are leaving?

ATHOS

Yes, but stay here.

PORTHOS

You undertake then?

ATHOS

I'm responsible for everything.

ARAMIS

Ought we to listen further?

ATHOS

Yes, if it can interest you.

(Leaving by the window.)

CARDINAL

(who has taken his cloak)

Well—it's agreed then, Madame.

MILADY

It's agreed, Monsignor.

CARDINAL

You have a post chaise?

MILADY

A hundred feet from here.

CARDINAL

Relays are ready on the entire length of the route—the sloop of Captain Felton is waiting for you—if you have a good wind you can reach London by tomorrow evening.

MILADY

I will be there.

CARDINAL

As soon as you arrive, you will send me news and tell me what you've done on the way.

MILADY

By whom?

CARDINAL

Don't worry about that—at the moment you need a messenger— a messenger will present himself.

MILADY

How will I recognize him?

CARDINAL

He'll say to you "La Rochelle".

MILADY

And I will reply?

CARDINAL

"Portsmouth"; you can give him your letter.

MILADY

That's fine, goodbye, Monsignor.

CARDINAL

Au revoir, Madame.

> *(Milady in her turn makes her preparations and she reads the decree.)*

MILADY

"It is by my decree and for the benefit of the state that the bearer has done what has been done—Richelieu—"

> *(speaking)*

No date—marvelous. With this, vengeance is sure and not dangerous.

> *(During this time, Richelieu has come down and rejoined his companions who leave with him—Aramis and Porthos stay on the first floor.)*

> *(Athos enters on the second floor and shuts the door after him.)*

MILADY

Who are you and what do you want?

ATHOS

To be together.

> *(He lets his cloak fall and raises his hat. Milady takes a step backwards.)*

MILADY

The Count de la Fère.

ATHOS

Yes, Milady, the Count de la Fère in person—who returns, express, from the other world to have the pleasure of seeing you again. Let's sit down, Madame and have a talk as the Cardinal said.

MILADY

(falling in an armchair)

Oh—my God!

ATHOS

You are then a demon on the earth? Happily, with the aid of God, men have sometimes vanquished the demon—you were already discovered on my way and I thought you were defeated, Madame, but I was deceived or Hell has resuscitated you.

MILADY

Ah.

(She envelops herself in her scarf.)

ATHOS

Yes, Hell has revived you. Hell has made you—Hell has given you another name—Hell has even given you another face. But it has not effaced the stain on your soul nor the brand on your body.

MILADY

Sir!

(She rises; Athos remains seated.)

ATHOS

You thought I was dead, didn't you?

MILADY

But now, what brings you back to me? What do you want?

ATHOS

I mean to tell you that while remaining invisible to your eyes—I haven't lost sight of you.

MILADY

You know what I have done?

ATHOS

Not only what you have done but what you intend to do.

MILADY

Oh.

ATHOS

You don't believe it? Well—listen up—you went to England—in leaving France you married Lord de Winter, Baron de Clarick—in about two years he died—of a singular malady which left blue spots all over his body. By his death you became the guardian of your son and the heir of Lord de Winter—then you returned to France and took up service with the Cardinal. It was you who brought to London the famous letter from the Queen which brought Lord Buckingham to Paris—it's you who brought the handkerchief to the Rue de la Harpe that was designed to cause the Duke to fall into a trap—it's you who, thinking to receive in your chamber the Count de Vardes, actually received the Cheva-lier D'Artagnan whom you wish ill, less for having surprised your terrible secret, than for not having killed Lord de Winter, your brother-in-law, of whom your son is the heir. It's you who now come to this room, seated in the same armchair in which you are now seated—it's you who has just taken on—from the Cardinal—the job of assassinating the Duke of Buckingham in return for the promise he gave you of permitting you to assassinate D'Artagnan.

MILADY

Then you are really Satan?

ATHOS

Perhaps—but in any case, listen carefully to this—to assassinate or not to assassinate the Duke of Buckingham is a matter of small importance. I don't know him, and besides, he's English— but don't touch with the end of your finger a single hair of D'Artagnan, who is a faithful friend, whom I love, and whom I will protect—don't touch someone belonging to him, or I swear it to you on the memory of my father, the crime you attempt to commit or shall have committed will be your last.

MILADY

Mr. D'Artagnan has cruelly offended me—Mr. D'Artagnan will die.

D'ARTAGNAN

Don't repeat that threat, Madame.

MILADY

He will die! He first—then she will follow.

ATHOS

Oh, take care—see the vertigo is overcoming me.

(he draws a pistol from his belt and coldly then icily)

Madame, you are going this instant to give back to me this paper you have signed by the Cardinal or—on my soul, I am going to blow your brains out.

MILADY

No!

(Aiming his pistol.)

ATHOS

You have one second to decide.

(Milady draws the paper from her bosom and lets it fall— grinding her teeth)

ATHOS

(picking it up and reading it)

"It is by my decree and for the benefit of the state that the bearer has done what has been done—Richelieu—"

(taking his cloak and his hat)

And now that I have pulled your teeth, viper—die, if you can.

MILADY

(twisted by rage)

Ah!

(Athos leaves the chamber.)

ARAMIS

What the devil can this woman be to Athos?

PORTHOS

I believe she's his aunt.

CURTAIN

ACT IV

Scene 10

The port of Portsmouth. On one side, Buckingham's tent—on the other, a type of masonry which can be used as a tavern by seamen. In between this masonry and the tent is a useable space where Milady writes in the tavern.

DE WINTER

(backing out of the tent)

Yes, Milord, it will be as Your Grace desires.

(calling)

Commandant of the Port.

CAPTAIN

(coming from a barge which is waiting with oarsmen)

Your Honor?

DE WINTER

His Grace, Lord Buckingham, will receive the officers of the Fleet this morning—then towards noon, he will go to the Admiral's flagship; this evening—we cast anchor.

CAPTAIN

Fine, Your Honor.

DE WINTER

What news?

CAPTAIN

A sloop arrived during the night.

DE WINTER

What nationality?

CAPTAIN

English.

DE WINTER

Commercial or war vessel?

CAPTAIN

Commercial.

DE WINTER

Captain?

CAPTAIN

Felton.

DE WINTER

Wait a minute—this Felton—isn't he an old officer of the Royal Navy?

CAPTAIN

Yes, Your Honor—discharged by Milord of Buckingham for insubordination.

DE WINTER

Did he bring passengers?

CAPTAIN

A woman—as to the rest, I shall have the honor to put under Mi-lord's eyes Captain Felton's log, which must be taken to and signed at the registry.

DE WINTER

Show me this registry.

CAPTAIN

I will bring it to Your Honor unless Your Honor wishes to come to my ship?

DE WINTER

I will go with you.

(They leave.)

(Milady, reading what she has written.)

MILADY

"Monsignor Cardinal, all has happened as Your Eminence has foreseen. The Captain of the sloop which has brought me to England is not only a brave sailor who made the transit in nine hours—but also an exalted Puritan, who prays to God each night to spare him from committing a crime and not to let him meet the Duke face to face. Felton during the crossing took pity on my sufferings—I told him without naming him that an English Lord had seduced me and shamefully abandoned me—and that the thirst for a terrible vengeance brought me to England—Felton cried with me and I've sung psalms with him. We call each other brother and sister—Cecily and Felton."

"Today, the 23rd of August 1624, the Duke has set up his tent in the port and hopes to get his ship in shape to set sail for France. I have arrived in time to tell Your Eminence that I believe he cannot get ready and I send this news hurriedly, to Your Eminence in our usual cipher. I wait in the meantime for Mr. Felton who, at nine in the morning must come to retrieve his register from the Port Commandant. It is 3:45—I have not yet seen the messenger that Your Eminence has promised me."

A MAN

(approaching her)

La Rochelle.

MILADY

Portsmouth.

MAN

I wait.

MILADY

You are leaving for France?

MAN

I go to whatever country you wish.

MILADY

You have means of transport?

MAN

A barque here—relays there—but you, Madame?

MILADY

It's as necessary for me as for you—A barque which at my order takes me from this port and can conduct me to the first fishing boat with which I can come to an understanding. There's the dispatch then—go—what are you doing?

MAN

(pointing to another individual who accompanies him)

This man leaves in my place.

MILADY

You have confidence in him?

MAN

As in myself.

MILADY

That's good then.

MAN

I remain at the order of Milady.

MILADY

Hang around the Duke's tent and try to understand me on a signal and to obey me on a word.

DE WINTER

(has returned to knock at a second compartment—to Buckingham who appears)

Your Grace was shut in.

BUCKINGHAM

(laughing)

Yes, I was saying my prayers—

DE WINTER

I didn't think Milord so devout.

BUCKINGHAM

Oh—I didn't say to what saint.

DE WINTER

Or virgin.

BUCKINGHAM

Hush! Let's not speak of the sins of our youth. Oh, the magnificent sea, the beautiful sky—my dear Lord.

MILADY

There he is.

BUCKINGHAM

You don't know how happy I am! I leave with a child's joy.

(At the appearance of the Duke the trumpets sound and the drums beat.)

DE WINTER

Do you hear, Milord, the sentinels who watch your tent made a signal and they're beating up the camp?

BUCKINGHAM

But that's a royal honor—de Winter.

DE WINTER

Eh! Aren't you the true King?

MILADY

Did he leave, by chance?

(she goes to the door)

And Felton never comes!

DE WINTER

Would you be pleased, Milord, to approach the end of the dock to see the fleet?

BUCKINGHAM

Yes—give me your arm, Milord.

CRIES

Long live Buckingham!

DE WINTER

You see this forest of masts, sir—you see this swarm?

CRIES

Long live the Duke of Buckingham, long live Milord Duke!

DE WINTER

Do you hear? Do you hear?

BUCKINGHAM

Thanks, my friends, thanks.

DE WINTER

Does Milord still have need of me?

BUCKINGHAM

No, my dear de Winter—give orders for the reception of my officers—and for the departure tonight, then return.

DE WINTER

In a half hour, I will be back.

(leaving)

BUCKINGHAM

(to Sentinels)

Don't keep anyone back—these brave people want to see me—is it a crime? Tonight, I am leaving for France. Let them know at least for whom they pray, and who may be going to his death for them.

CRIES

Long live Buckingham—long live Georges de Villiers—long live Milord Duke!

BUCKINGHAM

Thanks, friends, thanks! David, prepare my signatures—Patrick.

(Patrick approaches; the Duke speaks in a whisper to him.)

PATRICK

Fine, sir.

MILADY

(who is watching from her window)

Ah—what do I see down there? That black costume—that walk—slow and grave—it's him! He's very late coming—but there he is.

(low)

Felton! Felton!

FELTON

Someone call me?

MILADY

Yes—here—come—

FELTON

You, Cecily!

MILADY

I myself.

FELTON

What are you doing alone here? Why this pallor, this sparkling look—this open knife?

MILADY

(drawing him to the window)

Come here!

FELTON

Here I am.

MILADY

Look.

FELTON

That tent—I see it.

MILADY

Do you know the arms above it?

FELTON

Those of Georges de Villiers, Duke of Buckingham.

MILADY

I told you I had come to find an enemy in England.

FELTON

Yes.

MILADY

A man who stole everything from me—honor, future, fortune.

FELTON

This man—it was he?

MILADY

Can't you understand?

FELTON

Oh, the same who from me also has stolen everything: fortune, future, honor.

MILADY

Do I need to tell you again what I came here to do—and why this knife?

FELTON

No, I understand, I understand.

(taking the knife)

MILADY

What are you doing?

FELTON

In your turn—can't you understand?

MILADY

Felton! Felton! This man belongs to me.

FELTON

You are mistaken, for he offended me before you knew him.

MILADY

He is mine.

FELTON

He is ours—not a word! The Lord has brought me here by the hand. Praise be the Lord! I have the arm of a man, an offended man—and the dagger is better placed in my hand than in yours. Go back to the bridge and embark. And like the first sea bird that flies toward France you will bring the news of the death of the Duke of Buckingham.

MILADY

Oh no—to each his task. If I let you accomplish mine, Felton, it will not be to abandon you in your peril. I will not leave England without my friend—without my brother—without my hero— your sloop is under sail and awaits you. It brought us here—it will take us back.

FELTON

But, if God delivers me to the Philistines?

MILADY

Your sister is with you for eternity.

FELTON

Thanks—I am going to invoke the Lord—Sister, leave me alone in his redoubtable presence.

MILADY

Au revoir, my brother.

(she stops center back)

FELTON

Lord, you have judged the judge—you have condemned the tyrant, the number of his days is complete. Give me the strength to execute the sentence.

BUCKINGHAM

(kneeling)

My God, you have willed it that I must love uniquely in this world—the one whose image is here. Make me live, my God, so she will love me as I love her—make me die if I must be deprived of her love.

(Noise behind the tent, Milady comes in quickly.)

FELTON

Well, what's going on?

MILADY

A runaway horse. A man has just come in by the side—I don't know—but a Musketeer! I fear being recognized.

FELTON

Recognized?

MILADY

No—noticed.

(More noise.)

SENTINEL

I tell you, no one can pass—

D'ARTAGNAN

I tell you, I will pass, 'S'death, I intend to speak to the—step aside or if not—

FELTON

Do you hear?

MILADY

Yes, it seems I know that voice.

BUCKINGHAM

(on the sill)

What's wrong?

D'ARTAGNAN

Tell him it is a French gentleman who has killed three horses from Dover to Portsmouth—tell him my name if need be—Mr. D'Artagnan.

MILADY

D'Artagnan!

BUCKINGHAM

A French gentleman? Mr. D'Artagnan?

(leaving)

Here I am.

D'ARTAGNAN

Milord! Milord! Help—

BUCKINGHAM

Let him through. Let him through. Didn't I say that today all the world was free to come to me? You here, sir—I hope nothing bad has happened to the Queen?

D'ARTAGNAN

I believe not, Milord—only I know she runs a great peril from which only your Grace can save her.

BUCKINGHAM

Me? From the other side of the sea—I would be happy enough to be of some use to her—ah, speak, speak.

D'ARTAGNAN

Take this letter.

BUCKINGHAM

This letter—who is it from?

D'ARTAGNAN

From her.

BUCKINGHAM

From the Queen—my God.

(He staggers.)

D'ARTAGNAN

What's wrong, Milord?

BUCKINGHAM

(falling into a chair)

Oh, I hadn't expected such joy. Oh—I'll never see her again.

(reading)

"These diamonds or I am lost. These diamonds for love of her for whom you have suffered so much—Anne."

(speaking)

Let's see, my brave gentleman—what more do you know?

D'ARTAGNAN

Nothing—absolutely.

BUCKINGHAM

They're persecuting her?

D'ARTAGNAN

I think so.

BUCKINGHAM

But then you know?

D'ARTAGNAN

Yes, Milord, I know that it's twenty-five leagues to go from here to Paris—and that I have only twenty-five hours to make it.

BUCKINGHAM

In an hour you will return.

D'ARTAGNAN

Milord.

BUCKINGHAM

Oh—you must give me at least time to add a line to this box—
David, warn the admiral that I am putting the best sailing ship in
the squadron—the *Britannica*—at the disposition of this gentleman. Rest for an hour, Mr. D'Artagnan—for the love of your
Queen—one hour.

D'ARTAGNAN

There remain only twenty-three—Milord, take care!

BUCKINGHAM

Patrick, let them wait on this gentleman as if on myself.

PATRICK

Yes, milord.

BUCKINGHAM

*(leading D'Artagnan to the back takes the box from his
Prayer Stool)*

Here they are—these precious diamonds that I've possessed
which ought to follow me to the tomb—during eternity. She gave
them to me, she takes them back—her will, like that of God, be
done in all things.

PATRICK

His Honor is served.

BUCKINGHAM

Go, my dear Chevalier—while you drink a glass of French wine,
I will write her.

D'ARTAGNAN

Milord, I don't need to tell you I'd prefer you to give me my
leave a little sooner.

BUCKINGHAM

You've granted me an hour.

D'ARTAGNAN

So be it, Milord.

(to Patrick)

This way.

PATRICK

Yes.

(Leaving with D'Artagnan.)

BUCKINGHAM

Oh, my beautiful Majesty—to us both.

MILADY

He's alone now—he's writing.

FELTON

It's the hour—chosen.

MILADY

Go, Felton—go, savior of England.

(Felton descends and enters the tent.)

BUCKINGHAM

Who are you, and what do you want?

FELTON

Do you recognize me, Milord?

BUCKINGHAM

Ah, you are the young sailor I dismissed from the Royal Navy.

FELTON

The fault was light and the punishment heavy, Milord.

BUCKINGHAM

That's true—you come to reclaim—you come in at the right time, Felton, I am in a day of happiness. Your name will be reestablished in the cadres of the Navy—the second-in-command of the *Neptune* broke his leg yesterday—you will replace him, if you come about that—go.

FELTON

I didn't come about that.

BUCKINGHAM

And why did you come?

FELTON

To tell you, Milord, that you are about to undertake an impious war.

BUCKINGHAM

Beg your pardon?

FELTON

To tell you that it is neither the King nor England that you are protecting this time, but it is only your adulterous liaisons that you are serving.

BUCKINGHAM

Wretch!

FELTON

To tell you that the Lord wishes for you to renounce instantly—
this fatal war, which is the ruin of England and—then—then I
will forgive your past faults and in my name and those of my fellow citizens.

BUCKINGHAM

This man is mad.

FELTON

It's not a madman—it's only the matter of an insensate one who
pretends not to understand me.

BUCKINGHAM

Oh—withdraw, sir, or I'll call—and put you in a madhouse.

FELTON

You won't call.

BUCKINGHAM

Hey! Patrick, Sentinel.

(Felton strikes him)

Ah, traitor—you have murdered me.

PATRICK

Milord is calling me.

BUCKINGHAM

Help! Help!

PATRICK

Ah—murder.

FELTON

(escaping)

Step aside for the avenger of England—give way!

CRIES

(in the distance)

Ah—murder—after the assassin—run! Run—it's him, him, him!

MILADY

The boat, the boat—bring the boat forward.

D'ARTAGNAN

Milord! Milord!

BUCKINGHAM

Come, come, D'Artagnan.

D'ARTAGNAN

Help, a doctor.

BUCKINGHAM

Useless—useless—before the doctor arrives, I will be dead. Leave us—leave us—wait—wait—this box—here it is—it's all that I have from her—with the letter—the letter—where is it? Ah, let me kiss it once more, before my mouth freezes—that I may re-read it before my eyes close—D'Artagnan, you will give her this box.

D'ARTAGNAN

Milord! My God—if this murder were an enemy of the Queen— if he tried to assassinate me—I fear nothing for myself but I am taking this letter and this box.

BUCKINGHAM

Yes, yes, you are right—David—write—order to shut the port—not to let any boat leave, not even a skiff—for three days—except the *Britannica*, which will conduct Mr. D'Artagnan—give me, give me so I can sign.

(he signs)

David, this order to Lord de Winter. Go! Go!

D'ARTAGNAN

My dear Lord.

BUCKINGHAM

And now—quickly—quickly the box—my letter half written—good—you will take this box to Her Majesty and as souvenir.

(he shows him the knife)

Ah!

(falling)

No, no, leave me where I am—go—go, D'Artagnan and tell her that my last word was to pronounce her name—even my last sigh—ah, ah—her portrait.

(to David who reenters)

Well—the order?

DAVID

I took it to Lord de Winter himself.

BUCKINGHAM

Her portrait—thanks—thanks—leave, D'Artagnan.

SERVANTS

Dead!

GUARDS

(leading Felton)

Come, wretch, come.

FELTON

Dead.

MILADY

Dead—now—to France.

(a cannon shot)

What is that?

CAPTAIN OF THE BARK

Milady, the port is closed—the bark has been taken over by the Navy guard. Impossible to leave.

D'ARTAGNAN

Step aside! Give way!

MILADY

D'Artagnan.

D'ARTAGNAN

Oh—I quite suspected that this monster wouldn't be far away.

MILADY

Oh—at least he too will remain in England.

CAPTAIN

Mr. D'Artagnan, the *Britannica* is under sail and only waiting for you.

MILADY

You are leaving, D'Artagnan? Au revoir!

D'ARTAGNAN

Oh, Milady, oh cowardly assassin—yes, be calm. Au revoir, au revoir.

CURTAIN

ACT IV

Scene 11

A room in a hotel in Paris, in the back a gallery separated from the room by a large hanging. Aldermen—ladies—people of the court in the gallery.

TREVILLE

A Musketeer at this door.

(a Musketeer goes to take his post)

A French guard here.

(a guard takes his post)

JUSSAC

And now—a guard of His Majesty at this door.

TREVILLE

Excuse me? Sir? What are you doing?

JUSSAC

Sir, I am placing one of my guards here.

TREVILLE

Pardon—where are we, sir, if you please?

JUSSAC

Why, in the hotel, sir.

TREVILLE

And here to do what?

JUSSAC

We are coming to a ball, sir—a very beautiful ball that the Aldermen are giving for the King.

TREVILLE

And the King will be there, right?

JUSSAC

Surely, yes, milord since the ball is being given for him.

TREVILLE

Well, sir—especially as the King is coming—the King is at home—there can be no other guard than his guard—that is to say Musketeers, French guards and Swiss guards—a Swiss guard at the third door.

(a Swiss guard takes his place)

JUSSAC

Sir, I will complain to His Eminence.

TREVILLE

As you please, Mr. Jussac.

(Enter Rochefort.)

ROCHEFORT

(to Jussac)

And His Eminence will consider. You are wrong, sir, since Mr. de Treville is right.

(to Treville)

Sir, I am your humble servant.

TREVILLE

And I am yours, Mr. Rochefort.

ROCHEFORT

Beautiful party, Captain—beautiful assembly. How many flowers, how much gold and buffets! They're right to say Paris is the grand city—ah, it's a city of sweet jams and marmalade preserves.

TREVILLE

Who's this beautiful lady to whom they give a royal entrance?

ROCHEFORT

Madame President, sir, the mistress of the house. She will do honor to Her Majesty, the Queen.

TREVILLE

The Cardinal will come, I suppose?

ROCHEFORT

His Eminence is invited, sir.

(Noises in the distance.)

ATHOS

(to Treville)

Pardon, sir—the password.

TREVILLE

Don't let anyone into this hall except the King, the Queen, the Cardinal, and the great officers—

(pointing to a side door)

And into this room where the Queen will dress—no one except the Queen and her ladies.

ATHOS

Fine!

TREVILLE

Gentlemen, guards—gentlemen—Musketeers—! The King is coming.

(distant drums, music, acclamations)

(King entering from the back—the Cardinal by a side entrance)

ROCHEFORT

(to Cardinal)

Come this way, Monsignor.

CARDINAL

And they will dress here?

ROCHEFORT

The King in his cabinet at end of the gallery, the Queen in this room, facing Your Eminence.

AN USHER

The King!

THE KING

(center back)

Gentlemen, aldermen of my good city of Paris—I've come a bit late, excuse me, it's the fault of the Cardinal who detained me.

CARDINAL

(aside to Rochefort)

It's always my fault.

ROCHEFORT

Not this time, I believe.

THE KING

(uneasy)

Hasn't the Cardinal arrived?

CARDINAL

Sire, I was waiting for the moment to present my respects to Your Majesty.

THE KING

Ah, Cardinal, I blamed you to excuse myself. The fact is, gentlemen, that His Eminence prefers work to the ball—at what time will the ball begin, gentlemen?

ALDERMAN

As soon as Her Majesty, the Queen arrives, Sire, and after Your Majesty gives his order.

THE KING

My order! Oh, you are in your own home here—gentlemen—the Queen must be on her way.

CARDINAL

Her Majesty the Queen is better, Sire?

THE KING

The Queen is always sick when one believes her to be in good health, in good health when one believes her sick.

CARDINAL

But Her Majesty is coming to the ball?

THE KING

I'm expecting her to.

CARDINAL

She won't come.

(Noise—acclamation.)

THE KING

That must be the Queen.

USHER

The Queen.

(Enter Anne.)

ANNE

Good day, gentlemen.

(looking around her)

Nothing! Nothing! No one—No more hope. The Cardinal!

THE KING

Madame, I am excused by my work—but you, what excuse have you to be late?

CARDINAL

Madame.

(bowing, aside)

She doesn't have the diamonds.

(aloud)

Madame can give you a quite natural excuse—her beauty—the care of her toilet, the time taken to lace the sleeves with diamonds.

ANNE

Implacable as Hell!

THE KING

Why no! They're not there! Madame, why, if you please, haven't you your diamonds when you knew it would have been agreeable for me to see you with them?

ANNE

Sire—

THE KING

It's I who gave you the gift, Madame—I counted on seeing you appear in them—you've done wrong—

CARDINAL

They can be sent for—where are they?

THE KING

Yes—where are they?

ANNE

But at the Louvre—

(aside)

A little time, a little time, my God—

(aloud)

Your Majesty wishes.

THE KING

Yes, I wish it—for the ballet is going to begin as soon as the dancers are dressed, as soon as you yourself are ready.

CARDINAL

(aside)

Now from this point on she'll pretend a malaise—a fainting.

THE KING

Are you sending to the Louvre, Madame?

ANNE

I am going to send, yes—Sire.

CARDINAL

And I, too.

(he bows and leaves)

ANNE

You haven't had pity for me—my God! I am lost.

TREVILLE

If I can do something for the services of Your Majesty?

ANNE

You can do nothing, sir, nothing.

TREVILLE

Ah! Madame.

ANNE

Wait—do you know a guardsman—a young man?

TREVILLE

A young man?

ANNE

Who's called D'Artagnan?

TREVILLE

Who asked me for leave?

ANNE

You haven't seen him—he hasn't returned?

TREVILLE

No, Madame. Athos, you haven't seen Mr. D'Artagnan?

ATHOS

Mr. D'Artagnan? No.

ANNE

Then it's finished. It's over.

CHAMBERMAID

The service for Her Majesty.

(Queen is directed to her right—the ladies follow)

ROCHEFORT

(in the near center)

Gentlemen, gentlemen, a man has just come up by the little stairway—he forced the sentry post and overthrew the functionaries. They yelled to stop him but he pressured his way. Alarm! Alarm!

TREVILLE

A man?

ATHOS

A man? Let us see him.

D'ARTAGNAN

(enters covered with mud and dust—low to a guardsman)

Comrade—comrade—your musket.

ATHOS

D'Artagnan.

TREVILLE

D'Artagnan.

ANNE

(stopping in the doorway)

D'Artagnan! My God! My God!

ROCHEFORT

My Gascon—ah, it's you who overthrow the sentinels?

D'ARTAGNAN

My Thief! Me—what sentinels? I haven't overthrown anyone.

ROCHEFORT

Then what are you doing here?

D'ARTAGNAN

It's my turn of duty—I am taking my post.

ROCHEFORT

In this state—dusty—running with sweat? We are going to see if this is a—

ANNE

(low to Treville)

Oh—Mr. de Treville.

TREVILLE

(to Rochefort)

Sir—why are you meddling in this? Is Mr. D'Artagnan one of yours?

ROCHEFORT

No—but....

TREVILLE

It pleases me that a guard of His Majesty is covered with mud and sweat when he has run for the King—I believe that it is I who command here!

ROCHEFORT

That's so, sir, that's so—

(aside)

Oh, cursed Gascon!

(looking at D'Artagnan)

ATHOS

(to Rochefort)

Well, then?

D'ARTAGNAN

Let it alone, Athos—I have an open score with the gentleman.

TREVILLE

Your post is here, D'Artagnan.

D'ARTAGNAN

(low to Treville)

He's going to tell the Cardinal.

TREVILLE

I am going to accompany you, Mr. Rochefort.

(He leads him off.)

ANNE

Well?

D'ARTAGNAN

Here's the box, Madame.

ANNE

Ah—I am saved—my diamonds. Thanks! Thanks! A dagger—
Heavens, there's blood on this dagger.

D'ARTAGNAN

The blood of Georges de Villiers, Duke of Buckingham—who
told me as he lay dying to tell you—

ANNE

He is dead?

D'ARTAGNAN

In saying the name of Your Majesty.

ANNE

Georges! How costly it is to love a Queen.

USHER

(in the corridor)

The King.

ANNE

The diamonds—quickly—Estefana—protect this box.

THE KING

Well, Madame, have they returned from the Louvre?

CARDINAL

They haven't even been there.

THE KING

You are ready, Madame?

ANNE

At the orders of Your Majesty.

CARDINAL

(stupefied)

The Diamonds!

THE KING

Ah—you have the diamonds? Thanks. What were you telling me then, Cardinal on the subject of these diamonds?

CARDINAL

Nothing, Sire, nothing—

(aside)

How did they get back?

ROCHEFORT

Look at the dust which covers the uniform of this guard behind me—Monsignor.

CARDINAL

Ah—that's fine—come.

THE KING

(to Treville)

The Cardinal is very pale—do you know why?

TREVILLE

I believe I do, sir; it's a trick of the Queen—Your Majesty wishes to know it?

THE KING

Ah, speak.

ANNE

(to D'Artagnan)

How can I thank you for saving me—my hero—my friend?

D'ARTAGNAN

Not a single word, Madame—Constance has disappeared—where is Constance?

ANNE

To protect her from the vengeance of the Cardinal, I sent her to the Carmelites at Béthune.

D'ARTAGNAN

Thanks—I am paid.

ANNE

Ah—not yet.

THE KING

(to Treville)

So, the Cardinal has been tricked and he's enraged? That's very comforting.

(to the Queen)

I hope you will pardon me for the joke about the diamonds—won't you?

ANNE

(aside)

The joke!

(aloud)

Yes, Sire.

THE KING

You are coming, Madame? The ballet is starting—the music is lovely—

ANNE

(putting her hand on her heart)

Very lovely, Sire—

(She stifles a cry and gives her hand to the King.)

D'ARTAGNAN

The dead are happier!

CURTAIN

ACT V

Scene 12

A room in the convent of the Carmelites of Béthune.

SUPERIOR

You came to see the Superior of the convent of the Carmelites, sir—here I am.

ROCHEFORT

In fact, Madame, I have to ask of you some information.

SUPERIOR

Do so, sir.

ROCHEFORT

Did a women of twenty-four or twenty-five years coming on the route from Boulogne—stop in your convent?

SUPERIOR

But, sir, I don't know if I should reply to such a question.

ROCHEFORT

(pulling a paper from his pocket)

Order of the Cardinal.

SUPERIOR

I obey—ask, sir.

ROCHEFORT

Have you received, yes or no, Madame, at the convent of the Carmelites of Béthune—a woman of twenty-four or twenty-five years—coming on the route from Boulogne.

SUPERIOR

Yes, sir.

ROCHEFORT

When was this?

SUPERIOR

Yesterday.

ROCHEFORT

Inform her that a messenger from His Eminence is coming to speak with her.

SUPERIOR

She will be ready to see you in an instant, sir.

ROCHEFORT

Thanks.

(Exit Superior.)

ROCHEFORT

What the devil's her purpose in shutting herself up in a convent in Béthune? Doubtless to be near the frontier. A prudent woman, Milady de Winter.

(Enter Milady.)

MILADY

Ah—is it you, Count? Well—what has the Cardinal said about the death of Buckingham?

ROCHEFORT

Oh—he's in despair as a Christian—it's true that as a politician he can't prevent himself from saying it's a wonderful good fortune.

MILADY

And what has he ordered regarding me?

ROCHEFORT

He approves your project and sends me to you thinking you will have many things to tell me that you wouldn't want to confide to paper.

MILADY

He's right.

ROCHEFORT

Well—speak.

MILADY

The first is that while I'm waiting, I've found in this convent the little Madame Bonacieux.

ROCHEFORT

I suppose you've been careful not to show yourself to her.

MILADY

She doesn't know me.

ROCHEFORT

In that case, you must by now be her best friend.

MILADY

Precisely.

ROCHEFORT

And how are you taken here?

MILADY

I presented myself as a victim of the Cardinal.

ROCHEFORT

And the similarity of the situation?

MILADY

You understand.

ROCHEFORT

If I understand, I approve.

MILADY

As to the rest, your visit is going to do wonders.

ROCHEFORT

How so?

MILADY

In that you are going to say you have discovered my retreat and that they are coming to look for me tomorrow or the day after—I have reasons for not remaining at Béthune.

ROCHEFORT

Devil! But where will I find you if I need you?

MILADY

Wait—at Armentières.

ROCHEFORT

Fine. You haven't anything else to say to the Cardinal?

MILADY

Tell him that our conversation at the Colombier Rouge was overhead by three Musketeers of the King—that after his departure, one of these three men, named Athos, came up to me, and tore up the safe conduct he had given me; that these Musketeers must be feared, since they know our secret and that they must be gotten rid of.

ROCHEFORT

Are these three men the friends of our Gascon?

MILADY

Inseparable.

ROCHEFORT

Then they are the ones I met about three leagues from here—stopping at an inn.

MILADY

What do they want hereabouts?

ROCHEFORT

Didn't you say that one of them is the lover of little Madame Bonacieux?

MILADY

It's D'Artagnan.

ROCHEFORT

Well—without doubt, they are coming to find her.

MILADY

To find her?

ROCHEFORT

Yes, after the service that D'Artagnan has rendered the Queen—
the Queen cannot have refused her to him.

MILADY

You're right, Rochefort—it's not to Paris that you must return—
it's at Lille you must await me.

ROCHEFORT

Await you?

MILADY

Do you think the Cardinal wouldn't be very happy to have little
Madame Bonacieux under his control?

ROCHEFORT

Yes, but the Carmelites of Béthune are under the protection of
the Queen.

MILADY

And if I bring her to Lille?

ROCHEFORT

Oh—that's another matter.

MILADY

Then it won't be tomorrow or the day after tomorrow that I leave—it's today.

ROCHEFORT

In fact, our men could arrive from one moment to the next.

MILADY

You have a post chaise and a servant?

ROCHEFORT

Yes.

MILADY

Put them at my disposition.

ROCHEFORT

And I?

MILADY

You will go on horseback by way of preceding me to the hotel—Black Bear.

ROCHEFORT

That's where I must wait for you?

MILADY

Yes.

ROCHEFORT

At Lille—at the hotel Black Bear?

MILADY

At Lille—at the hotel Black Bear.

(Rochefort leaves.)

MILADY

Is it for her or is it against me that these four men are in the country? I don't know but, in any case, they won't find either her or me. Let's see—go to her and let's try to play our role of persecuted woman—ah—here she is.

MADAME BONACIEUX

Well, what you feared has happened, Madame? This evening, perhaps sooner—the Cardinal is sending to take you?

MILADY

Who told you that, my dear and pretty child?

MADAME BONACIEUX

But I heard it from the mouth of the same messenger.

MILADY

Come sit down, here near me.

MADAME BONACIEUX

Here I am.

MILADY

Wait while I make sure no one can hear us.

MADAME BONACIEUX

Why all these precautions?

MILADY

You are going to know.

(returning to her seat)

Then he played his role well.

MADAME BONACIEUX

Who's that?

MILADY

The one who presented himself to the Superior in the name of the Cardinal.

MADAME BONACIEUX

What—then this man wasn't—

MILADY

That man was my brother.

MADAME BONACIEUX

Your brother?

MILADY

Hush! Only you know the secret, my child, don't confide it to anyone in the world, or I will be lost and you, too, perhaps.

MADAME BONACIEUX

My God!

MILADY

Listen, here's what happened: my brother who knows that I was exposed to the Cardinal's vengeance came here to help me protect myself. He must have met an emissary of the Cardinal who came here to look for me—he followed him—took his sword in his hand to force the messenger to give him the papers he was carrying—the messenger tried to defend himself and my brother killed him.

MADAME BONACIEUX

Oh!

MILADY

Then my brother took the papers, presented himself here as the Cardinal's envoy and in an hour, a carriage will come to take me, sent by His Majesty.

MADAME BONACIEUX

Then you are going to leave us?

MILADY

Wait—it remains for me to learn from you news which will answer that question.

MADAME BONACIEUX

Which is?

MILADY

My brother has, moreover, discovered a conspiracy against you.

MADAME BONACIEUX

Against me?

MILADY

Yes, the Cardinal intends to take you.

MADAME BONACIEUX

Oh—in a convent, placed under the immediate protection of the Queen, he wouldn't dare to employ violence.

MILADY

No—but by trick.

MADAME BONACIEUX

Trick?

MILADY

Four emissaries of the Cardinal are en route intended for you.

MADAME BONACIEUX

What are you saying?

MILADY

Disguised like Musketeers.

MADAME BONACIEUX

Like Musketeers?

MILADY

While you were in the Queen's service—didn't you know a young guard or a young Musketeer, Mr. D'Artagnan?

MADAME BONACIEUX

Yes—without doubt. Well?

MILADY

They were going to come to the convent door in the name of Mr. D'Artagnan and ask for you—and when you crossed the threshold, they were going to kidnap you.

MADAME BONACIEUX

Oh! What do you advise me to do?

MILADY

There's a very simple way.

MADAME BONACIEUX

Which is?

MILADY

It would be to hide you in the neighborhood and thus make certain of any men who come to search for you.

MADAME BONACIEUX

But I have received a sure order from the Queen and they won't let me leave.

MILADY

Oh—a great difficulty!

MADAME BONACIEUX

Why?

MILADY

The carriage is at the door—you say goodbye to me—you stand on the stoop to hold me one last time in your arms—the servant of my brother who comes to take me is forewarned. He makes a sign to the postilion and we leave at a gallop.

MADAME BONACIEUX

Yes, yes, you are right. That way everything will go fine—all is for the best—but we must leave here.

MILADY

Yes, I understand.

MADAME BONACIEUX

If it was really D'Artagnan and his friends by chance?

MILADY

Poor little one.

(going to a service table)

You excuse me.

MADAME BONACIEUX

Oh—I beg you.

MILADY

You understand the carriage may arrive any minute.

MADAME BONACIEUX

Oh—how I tremble.

MILADY

(dipping a biscuit in a cup of Spanish wine)

Mad woman—! Oh! Do you hear!

MADAME BONACIEUX

What?

MILADY

It's the post chaise that my brother has sent for me.

MADAME BONACIEUX

They are ringing at the door of the convent.

MILADY

Go to your room—do you have some jewels you want to bring with you?

MADAME BONACIEUX

I have two letters from him.

MILADY

Well, go find them and come back to me.

MADAME BONACIEUX

My heart suffocates, I cannot walk.

MILADY

You love this Mr. D'Artagnan?

MADAME BONACIEUX

Oh—with all my soul.

MILADY

Well—think that in fleeing you are preserving yourself for him.

MADAME BONACIEUX

Ah—you give me back my courage.

(the door opens and a servant enters)

Who's that?

MILADY

Fear nothing—it's my brother's valet de chambre.

MADAME BONACIEUX

I am going.

(Exit Madame Bonacieux.)

SERVANT

Milady's orders?

MILADY

As soon as this young woman who just left gets near me in the carriage, you will leave at a gallop in the direction of Lille.

SERVANT

Is that all?

MILADY

Well, if during our preparations for departure you see three or four cavaliers appear, whip the horses—make the carriage turn around the convent and wait for us at the garden door. That's all—go.

(at the window)

It seems to me—no—nothing.

MADAME BONACIEUX

Here I am.

MILADY

Well, everything is ready, dear child—the Superior doesn't question anything—this man is going to give the last orders. Would you like to do as I am doing: to eat a biscuit and drink some wine?

MADAME BONACIEUX

No thanks, I need nothing.

MILADY

Then let's not lose an instant. Let's leave.

MADAME BONACIEUX

Yes, let's leave.

MILADY

You see—everything assists us—see, night's coming on.

MADAME BONACIEUX

Oh—what is that noise?

MILADY

Indeed.

MADAME BONACIEUX

It's the gallop of several horses.

MILADY

It's those or our friends or our enemies. Stay where you are. I will go speak to him.

MADAME BONACIEUX

(staggering)

Oh—my God! My God!

MILADY

It's the uniform of the Cardinal guards. Not an instant to lose—let us flee! Flee!

MADAME BONACIEUX

Yes. Yes.

MILADY

Come on then—but come on—

(one hears the carriage leave)

MADAME BONACIEUX

It's too late.

(One hears the cries—stop! stop! then two or thee shots.)

MILADY

No, we can flee by the garden gate.

(Madame Bonacieux falls to her knees.)

Oh, she will cause me to be ruined.

(she goes to the table, empties the contents of her purse in a glass and takes it, returning to Madame Bonacieux)

Drink—this will give you strength—drink.

(Madame Bonacieux drinks mechanically, Milady aside.)

This isn't the way I wanted to avenge myself—but one does what one can do.

(She runs from the room.)

MADAME BONACIEUX

(rising)

Wait here. I am….

D'ARTAGNAN

(in the street)

Queen's order.

MADAME BONACIEUX

(quickly)

His voice—it's his voice.

(running to the door)

D'Artagnan! D'Artagnan! This way—where are you, my God!

D'ARTAGNAN

Constance! Constance! Where are you?

(Enter D'Artagnan, Athos, Porthos, and Aramis.)

MADAME BONACIEUX

Ah! D'Artagnan, I no longer hoped—it's you then!

D'ARTAGNAN

Yes, yes—it's me!

MADAME BONACIEUX

Ah—how well I did not to flee with her.

D'ARTAGNAN

With her?

ATHOS

Who?

MADAME BONACIEUX

Why this woman, who from attachment to me, wanted to take me away, and who took you for guards of the Cardinal and who has just fled.

D'ARTAGNAN

The one who just fled! What are you saying? My God—a woman who's just fled?

MADAME BONACIEUX

What have I done? My head is troubled—I cannot see anymore.

D'ARTAGNAN

Help! Her hands are cold—she feels sick! My God—she's losing consciousness.

ATHOS

(examining glass into which Milady emptied her purse)

Oh, no! It's impossible. God will not permit such a crime.

MADAME BONACIEUX

Some water.

D'ARTAGNAN

Water! Water!

PORTHOS and ARAMIS

Water! A doctor!

ATHOS

Ah, poor woman! Poor woman!

D'ARTAGNAN

Now, she's coming to herself.

ATHOS

Madame, in the name of heaven, who's been drinking from this glass?

MADAME BONACIEUX

I have.

ATHOS

But who poured the wine that's in it?

MADAME BONACIEUX

She did.

ATHOS

The Comtesse de Winter, right?

ALL

Oh.

D'ARTAGNAN

(seizing Athos' hand)

What do you think?

ATHOS

She learned the retreat of this woman from the Cardinal and she came.

MADAME BONACIEUX

D'Artagnan! D'Artagnan! Don't leave me—you see quite well I am dying.

D'ARTAGNAN

In the name of heaven, run, call, ask for help.

ATHOS

Useless, for this poison there is no antidote.

MADAME BONACIEUX

Help!

(stiffening)

Ah—

(throwing herself on the neck of D'Artagnan)

I love you!

(she dies—Porthos weeps)

D'ARTAGNAN

Dead! Dead!

ARAMIS

Vengeance!

ATHOS

My God take pity on us.

D'ARTAGNAN

(falling near her)

Dead! Dead!

(Enter Lord de Winter.)

DE WINTER

I wasn't mistaken—there's Mr. D'Artagnan and his three friends.

ALL (except D'Artagnan)

Who is this man?

DE WINTER

Gentlemen, you are like me, in pursuit of a woman—aren't you?

ATHOS

Yes.

DE WINTER

Of a woman who has passed by here, seeing there's a dead body.

ATHOS

Who are you?

DE WINTER

I am Lord de Winter, the brother-in-law of this woman.

ATHOS

Ah, it's true, I recognize you now—you are welcome, Milord—one of us—but how?

DE WINTER

I departed five hours after she left Portsmouth. I arrived three hours after she went to Boulogne—I missed her by five minutes at Saint Omer, then at Lille I lost track of her—I went by chance, informing myself about the entire world when I saw you pass at a gallop. I wanted to follow you but my horse was too worn out to keep up with yours—and now despite your diligence—you have arrived too late.

ATHOS

(to the Superior)

Madame, we abandon to your pious care the body of this unfortunate woman—she was an angel on Earth before becoming an angel in Heaven—treat her like one of your sisters—we will return one day to cry at her tomb.

D'ARTAGNAN

(kissing her face)

Constance! Constance!

ATHOS

Cry! Cry! Heart full of love, of youth and of life—I wish indeed to cry like you.

D'ARTAGNAN

Now look—can't we pursue that woman?

ATHOS

Yes—right away—I have one last precaution to take.

D'ARTAGNAN

Oh—she will escape us, Athos, and it will be your fault.

ATHOS

I will answer for her.

DE WINTER

But, it seems to me, gentlemen—if some measures are to be taken against the Countess de Winter that concerns me.

ATHOS

Why?

DE WINTER

She's my sister-in-law.

ATHOS

And myself, gentlemen—she's my wife.

ALL (except D'Artagnan)

His wife?

D'ARTAGNAN

Oh—from the moment that you admit she is your wife, then it's certain she will die—thanks!

ATHOS

Be ready to follow me—in ten minutes I am here.

D'ARTAGNAN

And we shall leave.

ATHOS

Yes, but we need a companion for the way, and I am going to find him.

(A masked man appears at the door.)

MAN

A murder? She was here?

ATHOS

What do you wish?

MAN

I am looking for a woman who must have arrived here yesterday and whom I believed I recognized as she passed by my house.

ATHOS

That woman is gone.

MAN

(make a movement to leave)

That's well.

(Porthos and Aramis are before the door.)

ATHOS

What do you want with her?

MAN

That's my concern alone.

ATHOS

Pardon, sir, but as this woman has just committed a crime—it's proper that we assure ourselves about those she knows and those who know her; do you know her?

MAN

Yes.

ATHOS

Then you will tell me who you are?

MAN

You wish it?

ATHOS

Absolutely.

MAN

So be it. Approach me.

(whispers in his ear)

ATHOS

Ah—then be welcome.

MAN

How's that?

ATHOS

You are going to accompany us.

MAN

Impossible.

ATHOS

And why?

MAN

I cannot leave the town without a leave or an order.

ATHOS

Well—here's an order.

MAN

Signed "Richelieu."

ATHOS

Yes.

MAN

Command—I obey.

ATHOS

(to D'Artagnan)

Friend, be a man, women cry for the dead. Men avenge them. Come!

D'ARTAGNAN

And this companion for the road you lacked?

ATHOS

I've found him.

D'ARTAGNAN

Then—nothing more prevents us from pursuing this woman?

ATHOS

Nothing.

D'ARTAGNAN

(giving D'Artagnan a last hug)

Then let's leave!

CURTAIN

ACT V

Epilogue

A valley on the river Lys. Cabin to the right. Night.

MILADY

(alone in the cabin, looking at her watch)

Midnight soon—it's a league from here to Armentières—the master of the house has been gone only three quarters of an hour—the horses even with the greatest diligence cannot be here in less than twenty minutes. Patience, let's wait—

PLANCHET

(who is hidden facing the door)

Psst!

MOUSEQUETON

(appearing behind the house)

What?

PLANCHET

I heard her stir.

MOUSEQUETON

No, she's waiting.

PLANCHET

To our posts then.

(They retake their posts.)

MILADY

I seem to hear voices in the rustling of the wind, threats in the rolls of thunder.

(Grimaud rises on the height at the back and waves his handkerchief.)

(Athos appears followed by Porthos and Aramis, de Winter and by the masked man.)

ATHOS

Then you have tracked her down?

GRIMAUD

Yes.

ATHOS

Where is she?

GRIMAUD

There.

ATHOS

But she may have left this house; she may have taken flight?

GRIMAUD

There's only one door and one window—Planchet guards the door and Mousqueton the window.

ATHOS

(returning)

Come.

MILADY

It seems to me I hear some steps.

ATHOS

The owners of this house—where are they?

PLANCHET

This house was occupied by a butcher—overwhelmed by fatigue she was unable to go further—she sent the butcher to find post horses to Armentières.

ATHOS

And where is this man?

PLANCHET

We arrested him. Bazin is guarding him five hundred feet from here.

ATHOS

Porthos, to this door—me, to the window.

(to the others)

You where you are.

PLANCHET

I am here.

MILADY

(trembling)

Huh! This time I heard some steps on this side.

(she looks at the window and perceives Athos)

Oh—this is a vision, I hope.

(she intends to flee by the door)

PORTHOS

(raising his pistol)

Stop!

(Meanwhile, Athos has broken the window by a blow of his fist and entered into the cabin.)

ATHOS

Lower your pistol, Porthos—let this woman be judged and not assassinated—approach, gentlemen.

MILADY

(falling into a chair)

What do you want?

ATHOS

We want Charlotte Backson, who is called the Countess de la Fère, then Lady de Winter, Baroness de Clarick.

MILADY

You know very well that is me!

ATHOS

Fine—I wanted to hear this admission from your own mouth.

MILADY

What do you intend to do to me?

ATHOS

We intend to judge you, according to your crimes; you are free in your defense—justify yourself if you can. Chevalier D'Artagnan, to you goes the honor of being first accuser!

D'ARTAGNAN

(appearing on the sill of the door)

Before God and men, I accuse this woman of having poisoned Constance Bonacieux, who died within two hours in my arms at the convent of the Carmelites of Béthune.

ATHOS

Milord de Winter—your turn.

MILADY

Milord de Winter!

DE WINTER

(on the sill of the door)

Before God and men, I accuse this woman of having corrupted an officer of the Navy—named Felton and making him kill the Duke of Buckingham, a murder that at this moment Felton is paying for with his head. Assassin of Buckingham, assassin of Felton, assassin of my brother—I demand justice of you—and declare that if I don't receive it, I will do it myself.

ATHOS

My turn! I married this woman when she was seventeen years old—I married her despite my father. I gave her my wealth. I gave her my name. One day I perceived she was branded. This woman had a fleur de lys on her left shoulder.

MASKED MAN

(at the door)

I witness that.

MILADY

Who said "I witness that?"

MAN

I—!

MILADY

You! I defy you to find the tribunal which rendered this infamous sentence—I defy you to find the man who executed it.

MAN

(lifting his mask)

Here he is!

MILADY

(falling on her knees)

Who is this man?

MAN

Ah—you know me well.

MILADY

Ah—

ALL

You are—

MAN

I am the brother of the man she loved—whom she destroyed and who killed himself for her. I am the brother of Georges.

ATHOS

Chevalier D'Artagnan, what is the penalty you demand against the woman?

D'ARTAGNAN

The penalty of death!

ATHOS

Milord de Winter, what is the penalty you demand against this woman?

DE WINTER

The penalty of death.

MILADY

Oh! Gentlemen! Gentlemen!

ATHOS

Charlotte Backson, Countess de la Fère, Milady de Winter, Baroness de Clarick—your crimes have wearied men on Earth and God in heaven—if you know some prayer, say it, for you are condemned and you are going to die. Executioner—this woman is yours.

MILADY

You are cowards! You are assassins! You require six to assassinate one woman—take care!

ATHOS

You are not a woman—you don't belong to the human species; you are a demon escaped from Hell—and we are going to send you back there.

MILADY

Assassins! Assassins! Assassins!

MAN

The hangman can kill without being for all that, an assassin— Madame—he's the last judge, that's all.

MILADY

Yes—but for him not to be an assassin there must be an order.

MAN

The order? Here it is? "It's by my decree and for the good for the state that the bearer of this has done what he's done. Richelieu."

MILADY

Oh—I am lost!

ATHOS

Executioner, do your duty.

MILADY

(dragged by the Executioner)

Help! Help!

D'ARTAGNAN

Ah! I cannot see this frightful spectacle—I cannot consent that this woman be murdered thus.

MILADY

Oh! D'Artagnan—save me!

ATHOS

(between D'Artagnan and Milady)

If you take one more step, we will cross swords.

D'ARTAGNAN

Oh!

ATHOS

All you have the right to ask, Madame, is to die with our pardon—I pardon you the evil that you've done me—! I pardon you for my ruined future—my lost honor—my health forever compromised by the despair in which you have thrown me. Die in peace!

DE WINTER

I pardon you for the poisoning of my brother, the assassination of Lord Buckingham, the death of Felton. Die in peace!

D'ARTAGNAN

And I—pardon me, Madame, for having by an act unworthy of a gentleman provoked your rage—and in exchange I pardon you the murder of my poor friend—I pardon you—and I cry for you. Die in peace.

MILADY

Oh—last hope!

(to executioner)

Let's go.

(to Musketeers)

Beware! If am not rescued, I will be avenged.

(The Executioner drags her off.)

ATHOS

On your knees, gentlemen, and let's pray for a guilty creature who though pardoned is going to die.

EXECUTIONER

Come!

D'ARTAGNAN

Athos! Athos! Athos!

(One hears a scream cut off in mid-cry. The Executioner returns center back, naked bloody sword in hand.)

EXECUTIONER

Let the justice of God be done!

D'ARTAGNAN

(agitated)

All is finished. Pardon us, Lord!

CURTAIN

ABOUT FRANK J. MORLOCK

FRANK J. MORLOCK has written and translated many plays since retiring from the legal profession in 1992. His translations have also appeared on Project Gutenberg, the Alexandre Dumas Père web page, Literature in the Age of Napoléon, Infinite Artistries.com, and Munsey's (formerly Blackmask). In 2006 he received an award from the North American Jules Verne Society for his translations of Verne's plays. He lives and works in México.

250 / 24 - 16 - 85 - 74 - 59

2/1
29.9.
29.2
30. 1
26. 4
28.4

646 7+1
4 +55

47. 3

Made in the USA
Lexington, KY
24 October 2014